SAMSUNG GALAXY WATCH5 PRO USER GUIDE

Setting Up Device Pairing with Android and iOS Phones

AARON P. BONNER

COPYRIGHT

TABLE OF CONTENTS

INTRODUCTION

Introduction to Your Samsung Galaxy Watch5 Pro

The **Samsung Galaxy Watch5 Pro** is a cutting-edge smartwatch that combines functionality, style, and durability, setting a new benchmark for wearables. As a flagship product in Samsung's lineup, this smartwatch is designed for those who demand not only advanced technology but also ruggedness and high-performance capabilities in their devices. Whether you are a fitness enthusiast, an outdoor adventurer, or someone who simply enjoys having the latest technology on their wrist, the Galaxy Watch5 Pro is made to enhance your lifestyle, offering unparalleled features that seamlessly integrate with your daily activities.

With its sleek yet durable design, advanced health features, and long-lasting battery life, the Galaxy Watch5 Pro stands out as one of the best smartwatches on the market today. In this guide, we will walk you through everything you need to know about your new device, from the basic setup to the more advanced features, ensuring you can make the most out of every aspect of the Galaxy Watch5 Pro.

Overview of the Watch

The Samsung Galaxy Watch5 Pro is more than just a smartwatch—it's an all-in-one companion for fitness tracking, health monitoring, outdoor adventures, and connectivity. Featuring a sleek **titanium case** for added durability, a **1.4-inch Super AMOLED display**, and a **sapphire crystal** screen that provides superior scratch resistance, the Galaxy Watch5 Pro is built to withstand the rigors of daily life and outdoor activities. Whether you're hiking, swimming, running, or navigating your day-to-day tasks, this watch is designed to keep up with your busy lifestyle.

With a **49mm case size**, the Galaxy Watch5 Pro is designed for users who prefer a larger, more robust display. Its design combines style with function, ensuring that you never have to compromise on aesthetics for performance. The watch's interface is intuitive and user-friendly, making it easy to navigate through its wide array of features. Additionally, the watch comes with interchangeable straps, allowing you to customize its look based on your preferences.

The key to the Galaxy Watch5 Pro's success lies in its balance of style, performance, and ruggedness. While it's suitable for daily wear, it also boasts features tailored for the most demanding outdoor enthusiasts. If you're someone who enjoys exploring the outdoors, running marathons, or taking part in water sports, this smartwatch is built to be your perfect companion, offering everything from **GPS navigation** and **health tracking** to **long battery life**.

What's in the Box

When you open the box containing your Samsung Galaxy Watch5 Pro, you'll find all the essential components necessary to get started with your new device. Samsung ensures that the packaging is both simple and functional, with everything neatly organized to make setup a breeze. Here's what you can expect to find inside the box:

- **Samsung Galaxy Watch5 Pro**: The star of the show! This is the smartwatch itself, featuring a sleek titanium body and a sapphire crystal screen.

- **Charging Cradle**: The charging cradle is magnetic, ensuring your watch stays securely in place while charging. It offers **fast charging** capabilities, allowing you to quickly power up your device.

- **USB Type-C Charging Cable**: The cable connects the charging cradle to a power source, such as a wall adapter or a USB port on your computer. Samsung includes this standard cable to make sure you can charge the watch anywhere.

- **Interchangeable Strap(s)**: Depending on the model, you may receive one or two straps in the box. These straps are made from **fluoroelastomer**, providing durability and comfort. You can also buy additional straps to customize the look of your Galaxy Watch5 Pro.

- **Quick Start Guide**: This small booklet provides the essential instructions to set up your Galaxy Watch5 Pro and get started. It's perfect for those who prefer to have a physical guide at hand.

- **Warranty Information and Legal Documents**: These include product warranty details, safety information, and legal disclaimers related to the watch's use.

Having all these components readily available will ensure that you can begin using your watch immediately after setup, without needing to search for extra accessories or tools.

Key Features

The **Samsung Galaxy Watch5 Pro** is packed with a wide array of features that will appeal to different types of users. Whether you're looking for something to track your health and fitness or need a rugged smartwatch for outdoor adventures, the Galaxy Watch5 Pro has you covered. Below, we break down some of its most prominent features:

1. GPS and Outdoor Adventure Tools

The **Galaxy Watch5 Pro** is a perfect fit for anyone who enjoys outdoor activities. Equipped with **advanced GPS** capabilities, it allows you to track your location accurately while hiking, cycling, or running. The watch features **turn-by-turn navigation** and the **Track Back** function, which allows you to retrace your steps in case you lose your way. Whether you're navigating unfamiliar trails or need guidance in a new city, the Galaxy Watch5 Pro helps you stay on track and ensures that you never get lost.

2. Health and Fitness Monitoring

For those looking to track their health and fitness goals, the Galaxy Watch5 Pro is an excellent choice. It comes with a variety of health-related features, including:

- **Heart Rate Monitoring**: The built-in heart rate monitor tracks your heart rate throughout the day, during workouts, and while you sleep. This feature is essential for anyone looking to maintain or improve their cardiovascular health.

- **Sleep Tracking**: The watch provides detailed insights into your sleep patterns, helping you understand your sleep quality and offering tips to improve it.

- **Body Composition Analysis**: The Galaxy Watch5 Pro includes Samsung's BioActive sensor, which allows you to measure body fat percentage, muscle mass, and other key metrics. This can help you tailor your fitness goals to achieve better health outcomes.

- **Blood Oxygen and Stress Levels**: With the built-in SpO2 sensor, the watch allows you to track your blood oxygen levels, which is crucial for monitoring your overall health, especially during exercise. Additionally, the watch can monitor stress levels and guide you through relaxation techniques.

3. Battery Life

One of the standout features of the **Galaxy Watch5 Pro** is its impressive battery life. Thanks to its **590mAh battery**, it can last up to **80 hours** on a single charge under typical usage conditions. This long battery life is a significant improvement over previous Galaxy Watch models and makes the Galaxy Watch5 Pro an ideal choice for long outdoor trips, workouts, or multi-day adventures. Moreover, the **fast charging** feature ensures that you can power up the watch quickly, so you're always ready for your next activity.

4. Water Resistance and Durability

The **Galaxy Watch5 Pro** is designed to withstand the elements. With a **5ATM water resistance rating**, it's suitable for swimming and water-related activities. The **MIL-STD-810G military standard** for durability means that it can endure shocks, vibrations, and extreme conditions—making it perfect for those who participate in high-impact sports or outdoor adventures.

5. Connectivity and Smart Features

The Galaxy Watch5 Pro is more than just a fitness tracker; it also keeps you connected with your world. It features **Bluetooth, Wi-Fi**, and **NFC** for wireless connectivity. You can receive notifications for messages, emails, and app alerts directly on the watch. Additionally, if you opt for the **LTE model**, you can use the watch independently, making it perfect for those who want to stay connected without needing their phone nearby.

The **Samsung Pay** feature allows for contactless payments directly from your wrist, making it convenient for users who want to leave their wallet at home.

Getting Started

Now that you know about the features of your Samsung Galaxy Watch5 Pro, it's time to get started. Follow these simple steps to set up your watch and begin using it:

1. Charge Your Watch

Before you start using your Galaxy Watch5 Pro, it's essential to charge it fully. Connect the charging cradle to a power source using the included USB Type-C cable and place your watch on the cradle. Allow it to charge for at least 30 minutes before powering it on.

2. Power On the Device

To power on your Galaxy Watch5 Pro, press and hold the **power button** located on the side of the watch for a few seconds until the Samsung logo appears. This indicates that the watch is booting up.

3. Pair with Your Smartphone

After turning on the watch, follow the on-screen instructions to pair it with your smartphone. Download the **Samsung Galaxy Wearable app** from the **Google Play Store** or **Apple App Store** (depending on your phone's operating system). The app will guide you through the pairing process. Make sure Bluetooth is enabled on your phone and allow the app to access necessary permissions (such as location and notifications).

4. Customize Your Watch

Once paired, you can start customizing your Galaxy Watch5 Pro. Set up your watch face, adjust settings such as notifications, volume, and sound, and personalize your watch to suit your style. The Samsung Galaxy Wearable app allows you to manage watch faces, install apps, and tweak system preferences.

5. Sync Data and Start Using the Watch

The final step is to sync your data and begin using your Galaxy Watch5 Pro. Sync your health data, notifications, and preferences with your phone, and you're ready to start using the watch for fitness tracking, messaging, GPS navigation, and more!

The **Samsung Galaxy Watch5 Pro** is more than just a stylish smartwatch; it's a powerful tool for monitoring your health, enhancing your fitness routine, and exploring the world. With its durable design, advanced health features, and outdoor navigation tools, this smartwatch is built to withstand the demands of your active lifestyle. Whether you're hiking in the mountains or tracking your daily workouts, the Galaxy Watch5 Pro is your ultimate companion for every adventure.

By following this guide, you'll learn how to set up, use, and get the most out of your Galaxy Watch5 Pro. It's time to experience the future of wearables, one tap at a time.

CHAPTER 1

Setting Up Your Samsung Galaxy Watch5 Pro

The Samsung Galaxy Watch5 Pro is an impressive smartwatch designed to be both powerful and intuitive. Setting up the device for the first time is an easy and straightforward process that will unlock a world of health monitoring, fitness tracking, and connectivity. In this guide, we'll walk you through the entire setup process, from pairing the Galaxy Watch5 Pro with your phone to personalizing the device for your needs.

Pairing with Your Phone

Before you can start using your Samsung Galaxy Watch5 Pro, the first step is to pair it with your smartphone. The pairing process varies slightly depending on whether you're using an **Android** or **iOS** device. In this section, we'll explain the setup process for both platforms.

Pairing with an Android Device:

1. **Power On the Galaxy Watch5 Pro**:

   o To begin the pairing process, ensure your Galaxy Watch5 Pro is fully charged and powered on. Press and hold the **power button** located on the right side of the watch until you see the Samsung logo appear.

   o Once the watch powers up, you will be greeted by the welcome screen, and the device will enter pairing mode.

2. **Download the Samsung Galaxy Wearable App**:

   o On your **Android phone**, open the **Google Play Store** and search for "Samsung Galaxy Wearable." This is the official app you'll need to customize settings, manage notifications, and sync data between your phone and the watch.

   o Install the app by tapping the **Install** button.

3. **Launch the Galaxy Wearable App**:

   o Open the **Galaxy Wearable** app on your phone once it's installed. If it's your first time

16

opening the app, it will prompt you to start the setup process.

- o Make sure **Bluetooth** is enabled on your phone, as this is necessary for the connection to work.

4. **Select Your Device**:

- o Inside the Galaxy Wearable app, tap **Start** to begin pairing. The app will ask you to select your device model—choose **Galaxy Watch5 Pro** from the list.

- o A **QR code** will appear on your phone's screen.

5. **Scan the QR Code**:

- o On the Galaxy Watch5 Pro, you will be prompted to scan the QR code displayed on your phone. Follow the on-screen instructions on the watch to scan the code with its built-in camera.

- o The watch will then begin syncing with your Android phone. The process may take a minute or two.

6. **Complete Setup**:

   o Once the devices are paired, the Galaxy Wearable app will guide you through additional setup steps, such as agreeing to terms and conditions, signing into your Samsung account (if you have one), and selecting settings like notifications and permissions.

7. **Syncing Data**:

   o The app will begin syncing your data (including apps, contacts, and health information) to your Galaxy Watch5 Pro. Once the syncing process is complete, your watch is ready for use!

Pairing with an iOS Device:

The pairing process for **iPhone** users is similar, but there are a few differences due to the nature of iOS and Android operating systems. Here's how you can pair your Galaxy Watch5 Pro with an iOS device:

1. **Power On the Galaxy Watch5 Pro**:

   o   Just like the Android process, press and hold
       the **power button** to turn on the Galaxy
       Watch5 Pro and enter pairing mode.

2. **Download the Samsung Galaxy Wearable App**:

   o   Open the **App Store** on your **iPhone** and
       search for "Samsung Galaxy Wearable."

   o   Tap **Get** to download the app, and once it's
       installed, open the app.

3. **Launch the App**:

   o   Once the app is launched, it will prompt you
       to begin the setup process. Make sure
       Bluetooth is enabled on your iPhone for the
       connection to work.

4. **Select Your Device**:

   o   From the list of available devices, choose
       Galaxy Watch5 Pro. The app will then
       prompt you to confirm that you're pairing the
       correct device.

5. **Follow Pairing Instructions**:

   o After selecting your device, a **QR code** will appear on the phone. Follow the on-screen instructions to scan this code with your watch.

6. **Complete the Setup**:

   o Once paired, the app will guide you through final setup steps. This includes agreeing to permissions and notifications settings.

   o For iPhone users, it's important to note that some features, like advanced health tracking, may be limited compared to Android users, but the watch will still function well for basic fitness tracking, notifications, and other core features.

7. **Sync Data and Final Touches**:

   o After pairing is complete, the syncing process begins. The Galaxy Wearable app will update your watch with necessary settings, and once complete, your Galaxy Watch5 Pro will be ready to use with your iPhone.

Download and Install Apps

Once your Samsung Galaxy Watch5 Pro is paired with your phone, you can customize the watch to meet your needs. The **Galaxy Wearable app** offers an intuitive interface that allows you to manage settings, install apps, and personalize your watch.

Installing Apps via the Galaxy Wearable App:

1. **Open the Galaxy Wearable App**:

   o On your paired smartphone, open the **Galaxy Wearable app**. Here, you can access various settings related to your watch.

2. **Browse the Samsung Galaxy Store**:

   o Tap on the **Apps** tab in the app to access the **Samsung Galaxy Store**, which is where you'll find compatible apps for your watch.

   o Browse through various categories like fitness, lifestyle, entertainment, and productivity to find the apps that best suit your needs.

3. **Installing Apps**:

    o   Once you've found an app you'd like to install, tap on it, and hit **Install**. The app will be downloaded directly to your Galaxy Watch5 Pro.

    o   Some apps will require specific permissions to function, so make sure to review and approve any requests that come up during installation.

4. **Managing Installed Apps**:

    o   You can easily manage installed apps by going to the **My Apps** section within the Galaxy Wearable app. Here, you can remove apps you no longer need or install updates for existing apps.

5. **Installing Watch Faces**:

    o   In addition to apps, you can also install custom **watch faces** from the Galaxy Store. Watch faces are highly customizable, allowing you to change their look, data fields, and style to match your preferences.

o To install a new watch face, navigate to the **Watch Faces** section within the Galaxy Wearable app, and browse through the available options. Once you find one you like, tap **Install**, and it will appear on your watch.

Connecting Additional Services:

- If you plan on using services like **Spotify**, **Google Assistant**, or other third-party apps, make sure to link them in the **Galaxy Wearable app** or directly on your watch. These services may require additional account setup or authentication to sync seamlessly with your watch.

Navigating the Interface

The Samsung Galaxy Watch5 Pro offers an intuitive interface that is easy to navigate. Whether you're using the touchscreen, physical buttons, or swiping, the watch is designed for smooth interaction. Here's a breakdown of how to navigate the interface.

Touchscreen Gestures:

- **Swipe Up**: Swiping up on the screen brings up the **App Drawer**, where you can see all your installed apps.

- **Swipe Down**: Swiping down opens the **Quick Settings Menu**, where you can adjust features such as Do Not Disturb mode, battery saver, and more.

- **Swipe Left or Right**: Swiping left or right on the watch face allows you to switch between different screens or widgets (e.g., weather, heart rate, steps, etc.).

- **Tap**: Tap to open apps, notifications, and various menus.

- **Long Press**: Long pressing the screen allows you to access the **watch face settings**, where you can change the display style, layout, and other watch-related preferences.

Buttons:

- **Power Button**: Located on the right side of the watch, this button allows you to turn the watch on or off, open the **Apps Screen**, or return to the previous screen. It also functions as a **Home button** when navigating the interface.

- **Back Button**: The lower button on the right side of the watch lets you go back to the previous screen or menu.

- **Press and Hold**: Pressing and holding the power button allows you to **turn off** the watch or access the **Power Off** screen.

Personalizing Your Watch

Personalization is one of the best aspects of the Samsung Galaxy Watch5 Pro. Whether it's adjusting the brightness, changing the watch face, or customizing sound settings, there are many ways to make the watch truly yours.

Changing the Watch Face:

1. **Tap and Hold**: On the home screen, tap and hold the watch face until the **Watch Face Settings** appear.

2. **Browse Options**: Scroll through the available watch faces and tap on one you like. There are several customizable watch faces, ranging from digital to analog styles.

3. **Customize**: You can further customize the selected watch face by adjusting the complications (data fields such as steps, heart rate, weather, etc.) and changing the color, design, and layout.

4. **Download More**: If you want more variety, you can download additional watch faces from the **Samsung Galaxy Store**.

Adjusting the Brightness:

1. **Swipe Down**: Open the **Quick Settings** menu by swiping down from the top of the screen.

2. **Brightness**: Tap on the **Brightness** icon and adjust the brightness using the slider. You can also enable **Auto Brightness**, which adjusts the screen's brightness based on ambient light.

Personalizing Notifications:

1. **Settings**: Go to **Settings** in the Galaxy Wearable app or the watch itself.

2. **Notifications**: Customize which notifications you want to receive, such as calls, messages, apps, and reminders.

3. **Sound and Vibration**: Adjust sound settings and vibration patterns for different types of notifications. You can set different notifications to vibrate, ring, or mute depending on your preference.

Changing Language and Sound Settings:

1. **Language Settings**: In the **Settings** menu, you can change the watch's language by selecting **General** and then **Language**.

2. **Sound Settings**: In the **Sound** menu, adjust volume settings, choose from available ringtones, or mute the sound completely.

Setting up your **Samsung Galaxy Watch5 Pro** is an easy and exciting experience that opens up a world of customization and functionality. Whether you are pairing your watch with an Android or iOS device, installing apps, navigating the interface, or personalizing it to suit your preferences, the setup process is designed to be smooth and user-friendly. The watch's incredible features like GPS navigation, health tracking, and customizable options are all there to enhance your lifestyle, and this guide will ensure you know how to make the most of them.

By following these steps, you'll be able to set up your Galaxy Watch5 Pro with ease, customize it to fit your needs, and start enjoying all the benefits this premium smartwatch has to offer.

CHAPTER 2

Understanding the Health Features of the Samsung Galaxy Watch5 Pro

The **Samsung Galaxy Watch5 Pro** is not only a smart device designed for connectivity and convenience, but it also serves as a comprehensive health monitoring tool. Equipped with a variety of sensors and advanced technologies, the Galaxy Watch5 Pro offers users the ability to track key health metrics, such as **heart rate**, **sleep quality**, **blood oxygen levels**, **stress levels**, and **body composition**. These features enable users to take control of their health and well-being in ways that were once reserved for expensive medical equipment or specialized fitness trackers.

In this guide, we will walk through each of these health features, providing clear instructions on how to use them, what data they provide, and how you can leverage this information to improve your health and fitness journey.

1. Heart Rate Monitoring: How to Use the Heart Rate Monitor and Understand the Data

Understanding Heart Rate Monitoring

Your **heart rate** is an essential indicator of cardiovascular health, fitness levels, and how your body responds to exercise and stress. The **Galaxy Watch5 Pro** has an integrated **BioActive Sensor** that uses **PPG (photoplethysmography)** technology to measure your heart rate. By shining light through your skin, the sensor detects changes in the amount of light reflected by your blood vessels, allowing it to track the rhythm and rate of your heartbeats.

How to Use the Heart Rate Monitor

1. **Wear the Watch Properly**: For the most accurate heart rate readings, make sure the Galaxy Watch5 Pro is snugly fitted on your wrist. It should be positioned just above the wrist bone, with the sensors on the back making contact with your skin. A loose watch will result in inaccurate readings, so ensure it's comfortable but secure.

2. **Automatic Heart Rate Monitoring**: The watch continuously monitors your heart rate throughout the day. This is especially helpful for tracking how your

heart rate fluctuates during different activities, from exercise to periods of rest.

3. **Checking Heart Rate Manually**: If you want to check your heart rate at any time, you can manually open the **Heart Rate app** from the home screen. The watch will then give you an immediate reading of your current heart rate in beats per minute (bpm).

4. **During Exercise**: While working out, the watch will automatically detect your exercise session and provide real-time heart rate data. This information is crucial for ensuring you're exercising at an appropriate intensity for your fitness goals (e.g., fat burning, cardiovascular endurance, etc.).

5. **Continuous Heart Rate Tracking**: For those who want to keep a closer eye on heart health, you can enable continuous heart rate tracking. This setting will record heart rate data at regular intervals and store it in the **Samsung Health app**. To activate this, go to **Settings** > **Heart Rate** and select **Continuous Monitoring**.

Understanding the Data

- **Resting Heart Rate**: Your resting heart rate is the number of times your heart beats per minute while you're at rest. A lower resting heart rate is often a sign of good cardiovascular health and physical fitness. For adults, the typical resting heart rate falls between **60 and 100 bpm**. However, athletes and more fit individuals may have a resting heart rate closer to **40-60 bpm**.

- **Active Heart Rate**: This is the measurement of your heart rate during physical activity. Depending on the intensity of your workout, your heart rate will rise. Tracking this data helps you stay within your **target heart rate zone**—which can optimize fat burning, aerobic fitness, or high-intensity exercise.

- **Maximum Heart Rate**: Your maximum heart rate can be estimated using the formula **220 minus your age**. This is the upper limit of how fast your heart can safely beat during intense exercise. It's important to know your max heart rate to ensure you're not overexerting yourself during physical activity.

- **Heart Rate Variability (HRV)**: HRV measures the variation in the time between each heartbeat. Higher HRV often correlates with better overall health, as it suggests the body is responding well to stress and recovering effectively. HRV is an essential metric for those who want to monitor recovery and resilience to physical and mental stress.

Using Heart Rate Data Effectively

- **Monitor Your Fitness Progress**: By regularly tracking your heart rate, you can monitor your cardiovascular improvements. For example, over time, you may notice your resting heart rate lowers as your fitness improves, indicating that your heart is becoming more efficient.

- **Tailor Your Workouts**: Understanding your heart rate zones helps you customize your workout intensity for your fitness goals. For example, if you're looking to burn fat, you'll want to spend most of your time in the **fat-burning zone** (usually around 60-70% of your max heart rate), while if you're aiming for endurance, you'll want to be in the **aerobic zone** (70-80% of max heart rate).

- **Track Recovery**: Monitoring your heart rate after exercise helps you gauge recovery. A high heart rate that takes a long time to return to resting levels can indicate that you're overtraining or not recovering adequately. Conversely, a quicker recovery time suggests that your cardiovascular fitness is improving.

2. Sleep Tracking: How to Track Your Sleep and Interpret Sleep Quality Reports

Understanding Sleep Tracking

Good sleep is fundamental for physical health, mental clarity, and overall well-being. The **Galaxy Watch5 Pro** tracks your sleep patterns using motion sensors and heart rate variability, providing a comprehensive report on the quality of your sleep. Sleep is divided into various stages, and understanding these stages can help you make adjustments to your sleep habits.

How to Track Your Sleep

1. **Wear the Watch to Bed**: To track your sleep, simply wear the Galaxy Watch5 Pro to bed. Ensure the watch is comfortably snug but not tight, and that the sensors are in contact with your skin.

2. **Sleep Mode**: The watch automatically detects when you've fallen asleep and begins tracking your sleep. You don't need to manually start the sleep tracking feature unless you want to adjust settings.

3. **Check Sleep Data**: The next morning, after waking up, you can check your sleep data. The watch provides insights through the **Samsung Health app**, which will display details about your sleep duration, the various sleep stages, and your **Sleep Score**.

Understanding the Sleep Data

The **Samsung Galaxy Watch5 Pro** divides your sleep into several stages, each of which plays a unique role in your overall sleep quality:

- **Awake**: The time spent awake during the night. Waking up occasionally is normal, but frequent periods of wakefulness during the night may suggest poor sleep quality or sleep disturbances.

- **Light Sleep**: This is the lightest form of sleep and typically accounts for the majority of your sleep cycle. It is still restorative, but it's not as deeply restorative as the other stages.

- **Deep Sleep**: Deep sleep is the most restorative stage of sleep, where your body performs essential functions like repairing tissues, boosting the immune system, and releasing growth hormones. The more time you spend in deep sleep, the more rejuvenated you'll feel in the morning.

- **REM Sleep**: REM (Rapid Eye Movement) sleep is when you experience vivid dreams. It is crucial for memory consolidation, learning, and overall brain health.

The **Sleep Score** provided by the Galaxy Watch5 Pro is a numerical score based on how long you spent in each sleep stage and how many times you woke up. A higher score generally indicates better sleep quality.

Using Sleep Data Effectively

- **Improve Sleep Quality**: By tracking your sleep patterns, you can see how factors like bedtime, pre-sleep activities, or stress affect your sleep. Adjust your routine by minimizing screen time before bed or practicing relaxation techniques to improve your sleep quality.

- **Identify Sleep Disruptions**: If you frequently experience poor sleep or wake up tired, your data may show a lack of deep or REM sleep. In such cases, consider improving your sleep environment (e.g., noise reduction, temperature control) or consulting with a professional if sleep disturbances continue.

- **Set Sleep Goals**: Use the watch to set a goal for the number of hours of sleep you aim to get each night and the sleep quality you want to achieve. Tracking this over time can motivate you to maintain a consistent sleep schedule.

3. Blood Oxygen and Stress Monitoring: How to Monitor Your Blood Oxygen Levels and Track Stress with Guided Breathing Exercises

Understanding Blood Oxygen (SpO2) Monitoring

Blood oxygen saturation (SpO2) is a measure of how much oxygen your blood is carrying. It's an essential indicator of your respiratory health. The **Samsung Galaxy Watch5 Pro** includes an SpO2 sensor, which allows you to monitor your oxygen levels throughout the day and during workouts. Low oxygen levels can be an early indicator of issues like respiratory distress or sleep apnea.

How to Measure SpO2

1. **Launch the SpO2 App**: On the watch, open the **Samsung Health app** or the **SpO2 app**.

2. **Start the Measurement**: Ensure the watch is properly fitted on your wrist, and then follow the on-screen instructions. Sit still and relax for a few moments while the watch takes the reading.

3. **View Results**: The results will be displayed as a percentage. A normal SpO2 level is typically between **95% and 100%**. Anything below 90% may require medical attention, as it indicates that your blood oxygen levels are lower than healthy levels.

Understanding and Using SpO2 Data

- **Tracking During Exercise**: Monitor your oxygen levels during intense exercise. A sudden drop could indicate that your body is struggling to get enough oxygen, especially during high-intensity workouts.

- **Sleep Monitoring**: The watch can also monitor SpO2 levels during sleep. This is especially useful for identifying potential issues like **sleep apnea**, where oxygen levels frequently drop during the night.

- **Health Monitoring**: If your SpO2 readings consistently fall below 90%, it could be a sign of an underlying respiratory condition, and you should consult a healthcare professional.

Understanding Stress Monitoring and Using Breathing Exercises

The **Galaxy Watch5 Pro** also features **stress tracking** capabilities. By measuring changes in your heart rate variability (HRV), the watch can gauge how stressed you are at any given moment.

1. **Track Your Stress**: Open the **Stress app** to view real-time data on your stress levels. The watch will provide a percentage-based reading of your stress, with 0% being relaxed and 100% indicating high stress.

2. **Guided Breathing Exercises**: If the watch detects high stress levels, it will prompt you to engage in **guided breathing exercises**. These exercises help you slow your breathing and relax, which can reduce

cortisol levels and improve overall mental well-being.

3. **Using Stress Data Effectively**: By tracking your stress levels throughout the day, you can identify patterns that contribute to heightened stress, such as certain activities, environments, or lack of sleep. The data can help you adjust your lifestyle to manage stress more effectively.

4. Body Composition Tracking: Tracking Body Fat, Muscle Mass, and Hydration

Understanding Body Composition Tracking

One of the most valuable features of the **Samsung Galaxy Watch5 Pro** is its **body composition** tracking, which provides insights into your body's overall health beyond just weight. Using the **BioActive sensor**, the watch can measure several key metrics, including **body fat percentage**, **muscle mass**, and **hydration levels**. These data points are essential for anyone looking to improve their physical health and fitness.

How to Measure Body Composition

1. **Open the Body Composition App**: From the **Samsung Health app** or the **Body Composition app** on the watch, start the measurement.

2. **Sit Still and Relax**: For the most accurate results, sit still with your arm resting at your side. The watch will measure body fat, muscle mass, and hydration by sending a safe electrical signal through your body.

3. **View Results**: After the measurement is complete, you will receive detailed readings on **body fat percentage**, **lean body mass (muscle)**, and **hydration levels**.

Interpreting and Using Body Composition Data

- **Body Fat Percentage**: This metric is essential for understanding your overall fitness and health. A higher percentage of body fat can increase the risk of developing chronic conditions, such as heart disease or diabetes.

- **Muscle Mass**: Knowing your muscle mass helps track fitness progress, especially for those focusing on strength training. Increasing muscle mass boosts metabolism and supports fat loss.

- **Hydration**: Adequate hydration is crucial for physical and cognitive function. Tracking hydration helps ensure that you're maintaining optimal fluid levels for peak performance and recovery.

Using Body Composition Data Effectively

- **Track Fitness Progress**: Over time, the data allows you to monitor changes in body fat, muscle mass, and hydration. This is particularly useful for adjusting fitness plans to achieve a healthier body composition.

- **Set Goals**: If your goal is to decrease body fat, increase muscle mass, or maintain hydration, the watch's body composition data provides clear, actionable steps to guide your progress.

The **Samsung Galaxy Watch5 Pro** is not only a smartwatch with advanced connectivity, but it's also an invaluable health companion. With the ability to monitor **heart rate**, **sleep quality**, **blood oxygen levels**, **stress**, and **body composition**, it provides users with a comprehensive tool to track and improve their physical and mental well-being.

By leveraging these health features, you gain the insights needed to make informed decisions about your fitness and health goals. Whether you're a professional athlete, a fitness enthusiast, or someone simply aiming to live a healthier life, the Galaxy Watch5 Pro empowers you to take control of your health and unlock a better version of yourself.

Through regular tracking and smart goal-setting, these features work together to provide a holistic approach to maintaining a balanced lifestyle, ensuring you stay on top of your health and make the most out of every day.

CHAPTER 3

Fitness Tracking with the Galaxy Watch5 Pro

The **Samsung Galaxy Watch5 Pro** is a feature-rich smartwatch that offers advanced tools for fitness tracking, making it the ideal companion for individuals committed to leading an active lifestyle. With its powerful sensors, accurate tracking capabilities, and intuitive interface, the Galaxy Watch5 Pro is designed to track everything from everyday activities to specific workouts and outdoor adventures. In this comprehensive guide, we will explore how to use the fitness tracking features of the Galaxy Watch5 Pro, including **activity tracking**, **workouts and exercise modes**, **GPS navigation for outdoor activities**, and **tracking progress** over time.

1. Activity Tracking: How to Track Steps, Calories Burned, and Distance Traveled

The **activity tracking** feature of the Samsung Galaxy Watch5 Pro allows you to track your movement and gain insights into how active you are throughout the day. Whether you're walking, running, or simply going about your daily tasks, this feature can provide valuable data to help you stay on track with your fitness goals.

How to Track Steps

1. **Automatic Step Tracking**: The **Galaxy Watch5 Pro** automatically tracks your steps throughout the day. As long as you're wearing the watch, it will measure the number of steps you take and sync that data to the **Samsung Health app** on your phone.

2. **Checking Your Step Count**: To check your step count, simply swipe up on the main screen to access the **App Drawer** and tap the **Samsung Health app**. Under the **Activity** section, you'll see your daily step count.

3. **Setting a Step Goal**: You can set a personalized step goal for the day to stay motivated. To do this:

   o Open the **Samsung Health app** on the watch.

   o Scroll to the **Steps** section and tap on the **three dots** at the top-right corner.

   o Select **Set Goal**, and enter your desired step target for the day. The watch will alert you as you approach or meet your goal.

4. **Achieving Milestones**: You can also track your progress toward your step goal in real-time, with periodic reminders or cheers when you hit milestones. This can be an excellent motivator to stay active throughout the day.

How to Track Calories Burned

1. **Calories Burned in Real Time**: The Galaxy Watch5 Pro uses both heart rate data and activity levels to estimate how many calories you burn throughout the day. It takes into account both **active calories** (burned through exercise and movement) and **resting calories** (burned while at rest).

2. **Viewing Your Calorie Burn**: To see how many calories you've burned, open the **Samsung Health app** on the watch or your smartphone. In the app, you'll find the calorie count for each day, and you can track your total calories burned alongside other metrics like steps and activity minutes.

3. **Calories Burned During Activities**: The watch will also display how many calories you've burned during specific activities, like walking or running. This is useful for tracking the effectiveness of your

workouts and comparing calorie burn across different sessions.

Tracking Distance Traveled

1. **Automatic Distance Tracking**: The **Galaxy Watch5 Pro** automatically tracks the distance you travel based on the number of steps you take and your stride length. This allows the watch to give you an estimate of how far you've walked or run during the day.

2. **Measuring Distance During Specific Activities**: When you're engaged in activities like **running**, **cycling**, or **walking**, the watch tracks your distance in real-time by combining data from its **accelerometer** and **GPS**. The distance traveled is displayed on your watch screen during the activity and saved in your fitness log.

3. **Using GPS for Accurate Distance Measurement**: If you're exercising outdoors and want precise distance tracking (such as when running or cycling), the **GPS feature** can be enabled for accurate measurements, as we'll explore in the next section.

2. Workouts and Exercise Modes: Explore the Available Workout Modes and How to Set Goals and Track Progress

The Galaxy Watch5 Pro supports a wide range of **workout modes** designed for different activities. Whether you're running, cycling, swimming, or engaging in strength training, the watch provides tailored tracking to help you achieve your fitness goals.

Available Workout Modes

The **Galaxy Watch5 Pro** offers over **90 workout modes**, covering a variety of sports and activities. Some of the most common modes include:

1. **Running**: This mode is designed for both outdoor and indoor running. It tracks your pace, distance, and time, as well as advanced metrics like your **cadence**, **stride length**, and **elevation**. The watch also provides real-time voice prompts to keep you motivated throughout your run.

2. **Cycling**: Whether you're cycling outdoors or on a stationary bike, the watch tracks metrics such as speed, distance, and elevation gain. The GPS function can be used for outdoor cycling to map your

route, while the heart rate monitor provides data on your cardiovascular effort.

3. **Swimming**: The **Galaxy Watch5 Pro** is **5ATM water-resistant**, allowing you to use it for swim tracking. It tracks your laps, stroke type, stroke count, and the total distance swum. It even measures your **SWOLF score** (a combination of stroke count and time), which helps you gauge your swimming efficiency.

4. **Strength Training**: The watch tracks strength training exercises by detecting motion through its accelerometer. It automatically counts repetitions and sets and monitors your rest periods. The **repetition counter** feature is particularly useful when performing exercises like squats, bench presses, or bicep curls.

5. **Walking**: This mode allows you to track walking activity, similar to running but with a lower intensity. It tracks time, distance, and calories burned, and you can set personal walking goals for each session.

6. **Other Modes**: Other modes include yoga, pilates, hiking, rowing, and elliptical workouts. Each of

these modes is tailored to the specific exercise and offers metrics that are relevant to that activity.

Setting Fitness Goals

1. **Set Goals for Each Activity**: You can set personalized goals for different activities, such as distance, time, or calorie burn. For instance, if you're running, you can set a goal for the distance you want to cover. Similarly, if you're cycling, you can set a time-based goal for how long you want to ride.

2. **Track Progress in Real-Time**: As you engage in your workout, the **Galaxy Watch5 Pro** provides real-time feedback, including a visual display of your progress toward your set goals. This can help you stay focused and motivated during the workout.

3. **Challenge Yourself**: If you're looking to push your limits, consider using the **Samsung Health app** to track long-term goals. You can set monthly or yearly goals for steps, calories, or exercise minutes, and the app will keep track of your progress.

Tracking Workout Progress

1. **Post-Workout Summary**: After completing your workout, the Galaxy Watch5 Pro will provide a detailed summary that includes:

   o **Time spent** in the workout.

   o **Calories burned** during the session.

   o **Distance covered** (for running, cycling, walking).

   o **Heart rate zone data** showing how long you spent in different intensity zones.

   o **Pace and speed** (for running and cycling).

   o **Elevation gain** (for outdoor workouts).

2. **Fitness Insights**: The Samsung Health app offers insights and trends based on your workouts. You can track your progress over time, identify areas of improvement, and adjust your training plan accordingly.

3. **Tracking Performance Over Time**: Over time, you can compare your workouts from previous sessions and see improvements in key areas like distance,

speed, calories burned, or heart rate performance. This allows you to see how much progress you're making and whether you're on track to achieve your fitness goals.

3. GPS Navigation for Outdoor Activities: Guide on Using the Built-In GPS for Activities like Hiking, Running, and Cycling

One of the most powerful features of the **Galaxy Watch5 Pro** is its **built-in GPS**, which allows you to track your route during outdoor activities such as running, cycling, or hiking. The GPS functionality is accurate and can map your path, distance, and even the elevation changes during your workout.

Using GPS for Outdoor Activities

1. **Enable GPS Tracking**:

   o Before starting your outdoor workout, make sure that GPS is enabled. Open the **Samsung Health app** or select the specific workout mode (e.g., running or cycling) on the watch. GPS will automatically turn on during these activities, but you can manually enable it through the settings.

2. **Start Tracking Your Activity**:

    o   For running, hiking, or cycling, once you start the workout, the GPS will track your movement and create a map of your route. The watch will display your real-time location, distance, and pace as you move along.

3. **View Your Route**:

    o   After your workout, you can view the map of your route on your watch or in the **Samsung Health app**. This will show you where you went, how far you traveled, and the total distance you covered.

4. **Elevation Tracking**:

    o   For outdoor activities like hiking, the **Galaxy Watch5 Pro** uses GPS data along with an **altimeter** to track changes in elevation. This provides useful information for those tackling steep hills or mountainous terrain.

5. **Track Back**:

   o If you're out hiking or cycling and want to retrace your steps, the **Track Back** feature in the Galaxy Watch5 Pro helps you find your way back to your starting point. It records your route in real-time and can guide you back to where you started in case you get lost.

Using GPS for Accuracy

The GPS functionality in the Galaxy Watch5 Pro is highly accurate, making it perfect for runners and cyclists who want precise data on their distance and pace. The watch also integrates with the **Samsung Health app** to give you detailed route maps and performance stats after each workout.

4. Tracking Progress and Reviewing Data: How to Check Your Fitness Achievements and Use Samsung Health for Ongoing Health Insights

The **Samsung Health app** is your central hub for reviewing all of your fitness and health data. After completing workouts or activities, you can check your progress and gain insights that will help you adjust your fitness journey.

Viewing Your Progress

1. **Post-Workout Summaries**:

   o   After each workout, you'll receive a detailed summary on the Galaxy Watch5 Pro or the **Samsung Health app**, which includes all relevant metrics such as heart rate, calories burned, distance, time, and more.

2. **Historical Data**:

   o   In **Samsung Health**, you can review your historical workout data to track long-term progress. The app organizes data by activity type (e.g., running, cycling, strength training) and displays metrics like weekly totals, averages, and improvements over time.

3. **Achievements and Challenges**:

   o   Samsung Health also provides motivational features such as **badges** for achieving fitness milestones (e.g., completing a certain number of workouts or steps) and **challenges** to encourage you to stay consistent with your fitness goals. You can set weekly or monthly goals for yourself and see your progress in real-time.

Long-Term Health Insights

1. **Fitness Tracking Overview**:

   o The Samsung Health app provides a comprehensive overview of your health data, including **activity minutes**, **steps**, **workouts**, and **calories burned**. This enables you to track your overall fitness progress and understand where improvements are needed.

2. **Trends and Patterns**:

   o By consistently tracking your activities, Samsung Health gives you a clear picture of your fitness trends. Are you exercising more frequently? Are your calorie burns increasing? These insights help you identify where you need to adjust your training.

3. **Customizing Reports**:

   o You can customize the data displayed in the app to focus on the metrics that matter most to you, whether that's tracking calories burned, steps taken, or exercise duration.

The **Samsung Galaxy Watch5 Pro** is an exceptional tool for anyone committed to improving their fitness and health. Its advanced **fitness tracking features**, including **activity tracking, workouts and exercise modes, GPS navigation**, and **tracking progress**, make it easy to monitor your fitness journey in real-time.

By consistently tracking your workouts and daily activities, you can gain valuable insights into your progress, set new goals, and stay motivated on your path to a healthier lifestyle. Whether you're an avid runner, a casual gym-goer, or someone just looking to stay active, the Galaxy Watch5 Pro offers all the features you need to take control of your health and fitness in an intuitive, comprehensive way.

With the data and insights provided by the watch and the **Samsung Health app**, you can refine your workouts, track your achievements, and make more informed decisions to improve your fitness over time. This is truly a smartwatch that goes beyond just telling time—it's a comprehensive fitness and health companion.

CHAPTER 4

Advanced Outdoor Features for Adventurers

For adventurers, fitness enthusiasts, and those who enjoy spending time in nature, the **Samsung Galaxy Watch5 Pro** offers an exceptional suite of **outdoor features** that make it an indispensable tool for navigating trails, tracking progress, and exploring the great outdoors. From **route and turn-by-turn navigation** to **altitude and elevation tracking**, the Galaxy Watch5 Pro is equipped with powerful tools designed to enhance your outdoor experiences, whether you're hiking, biking, running, or even playing a round of golf.

In this guide, we will cover the **advanced outdoor features** of the Galaxy Watch5 Pro, providing you with the knowledge needed to fully utilize the watch's navigation, tracking, and sports-specific tools. Whether you're venturing into the mountains, navigating through city streets, or perfecting your golf game, the Galaxy Watch5 Pro ensures you're always prepared for your next adventure.

1. Route and Turn-By-Turn Navigation: How to Use the Galaxy Watch5 Pro for Navigating Trails, Parks, and City Streets

One of the standout features of the **Galaxy Watch5 Pro** is its **route and turn-by-turn navigation**, which makes it an essential tool for adventurers who love to explore unfamiliar terrain. Whether you're out on a hiking trail, biking through the city, or running in a new neighborhood, the watch's built-in GPS and mapping capabilities allow you to navigate with ease.

How to Use Route and Turn-By-Turn Navigation

1. **Prepare Your Route Using Your Smartphone**:

   o The first step in using the **turn-by-turn navigation** feature is to plan your route. Open the **Samsung Health app** on your smartphone or use a third-party app like **Komoot** or **Strava** to create a route, whether it's for hiking, running, or cycling.

   o If you're planning an outdoor activity such as a hike or a trail run, you can input the desired location into the app to generate a route. The **Samsung Health app** or the **Google Maps**

app also allows you to view a map of your area, helping you select your desired route.

2. **Send the Route to Your Galaxy Watch5 Pro**:

   ○ Once your route is created, send it to your **Galaxy Watch5 Pro** via Bluetooth. You can sync the route directly through the Samsung Health app, or if you're using an alternative third-party app, ensure it is compatible with your device.

   ○ Open the **Samsung Health app** on your watch, and navigate to **Route Navigation** under the **Exercise** section. Your watch will display a map with your current location and the planned route.

3. **Turn-By-Turn Navigation**:

   ○ As you start your activity, the **Galaxy Watch5 Pro** will display turn-by-turn directions directly on the screen. These directions will be presented with easy-to-read visual prompts and vibrations, notifying you when to make a turn or change direction. The watch uses GPS to track your location and keeps you on course.

- o For **running and cycling**, the watch provides continuous updates on your pace, distance, and remaining route distance, while showing the next direction you should take.

4. **Using the Watch for Real-Time Tracking**:

- o The watch will show a live map, allowing you to monitor your progress throughout the activity. This feature is particularly helpful when navigating trails or in areas where you don't have a clear view of your surroundings. If you're hiking in a dense forest or on winding trails, the **turn-by-turn navigation** ensures that you stay on course.

- o Additionally, the watch provides real-time information about your route, including **distance to the next turn**, **time to destination**, and **remaining distance**.

5. **Use the Galaxy Watch5 Pro for City Navigation**:

- o Beyond the wilderness, the **turn-by-turn navigation** feature can be extremely useful for urban activities like running, biking, or even walking in a new city. When navigating city streets, the watch uses **Google Maps** or **Samsung Maps** for precise directions. The watch will vibrate when you need to make a turn and display the relevant information clearly on the screen.

Key Benefits of Route and Turn-By-Turn Navigation

- **Hands-Free Navigation**: The **Galaxy Watch5 Pro** allows you to focus on your activity without having to pull out your phone for directions.

- **Outdoor Adventure-Friendly**: The built-in **GPS functionality** ensures that you stay on the right track in remote areas, including hiking trails or off-road routes.

- **Real-Time Updates**: You get continuous updates about your progress, helping you stay oriented and avoid getting lost during your journey.

2. Track Back Feature: Guide on How the Watch Helps You Retrace Your Steps During Hiking or Outdoor Activities

Getting lost during outdoor activities can be a frustrating and potentially dangerous experience, especially in unfamiliar terrain. Fortunately, the **Track Back** feature on the **Galaxy Watch5 Pro** is designed to help you retrace your steps, providing a safety net in case you need to find your way back to your starting point.

How to Use the Track Back Feature

1. **Start Your Activity**:

   o Begin your hike, run, or bike ride as usual, ensuring the **GPS feature** is enabled for accurate tracking.

   o As you move along the trail or route, your **Galaxy Watch5 Pro** will record your path in real-time using its GPS.

2. **Activate Track Back**:

   o If at any point you feel unsure of your direction or if you're simply ready to return to your starting point, open the **Samsung Health app** or the **Route Navigation** app on your watch.

o   Select the **Track Back** option. The watch will immediately activate the feature and display the route you took, allowing you to retrace your steps back to the starting point.

3. **Following the Track**:

   o   The watch will guide you back using the same route you followed initially, showing a map with arrows indicating the direction you need to go. The feature will provide continuous updates to ensure you're on the right track.

   o   If you made any deviations along the way, the watch will correct your course, ensuring that you're always on track to return safely.

4. **Tracking Elevation**:

   o   The **Track Back feature** also works in conjunction with **altitude tracking**, so if you're hiking in mountainous terrain, the watch will help you retrace your steps at varying elevations. The **altimeter** will ensure you are following the correct path, even if the terrain changes.

Key Benefits of Track Back

- **Safety**: It helps ensure that you can always find your way back, especially if you're hiking in areas with poor cell reception.

- **Peace of Mind**: You can confidently explore remote trails knowing that your watch can guide you back to safety.

- **Accurate Routing**: The watch keeps a precise record of your movements, ensuring that you retrace the exact path you took, reducing the risk of getting lost.

3. Altitude and Elevation Tracking: How to Measure Altitude and Track Elevation Changes During Outdoor Activities

Whether you're hiking, cycling, or running on uneven terrain, **altitude** and **elevation changes** are critical metrics for understanding the difficulty of your activity and assessing your physical performance. The **Galaxy Watch5 Pro** includes an integrated **barometric altimeter** that tracks your altitude and elevation gain/loss during outdoor activities, making it easier to assess the terrain and adjust your efforts accordingly.

How to Track Altitude and Elevation Changes

1. **Activate the Altimeter**:

   o The **altimeter** is automatically activated when you begin any outdoor activity, such as hiking, running, or cycling.

   o If you're navigating through an area with significant elevation changes (e.g., mountain trails), the **Galaxy Watch5 Pro** will automatically track these fluctuations using the built-in **barometric sensor**.

2. **Monitor Elevation Gain and Loss**:

   o As you hike or cycle, your watch will display your **current altitude** and the **total elevation gain/loss**. This is particularly useful for hikers or cyclists who want to track their performance and understand how much of a climb or descent they've completed.

   o You can view this information in real-time on your watch, which will show your **altitude in meters or feet**.

3. **Check Your Elevation Progress**:

   o If you're tackling a challenging mountain trail or a steep hill, you'll see the **elevation gain** as you ascend. This can help you pace yourself and set realistic goals for completing the route.

   o Once you reach your destination, you'll have a record of the total elevation gain during your activity, which can serve as a gauge for your fitness level and endurance.

4. **Post-Activity Elevation Data**:

   o After completing your outdoor activity, you can review the **elevation data** in the **Samsung Health app**. The app will provide a detailed breakdown of your total **elevation gain/loss**, along with a map of your route and elevation profile.

   o This is particularly useful for tracking progress on climbing challenges or for assessing how much physical effort you put into a particular workout.

Key Benefits of Altitude and Elevation Tracking

- **Performance Insight**: Tracking elevation helps you assess how challenging a route is, which can inform your future workouts or training sessions.

- **Accurate Terrain Mapping**: For adventurers and hikers, knowing the altitude and elevation changes is crucial for understanding the terrain.

- **Improved Fitness**: Elevation tracking allows you to set specific fitness goals related to climbing, improving endurance, or training for mountainous terrain.

4. Golf Mode: Step-by-Step Guide on How to Use Golf Mode, Including Accessing Course Maps and Tracking Your Game

For golf enthusiasts, the **Galaxy Watch5 Pro** offers a specialized **Golf Mode** that enhances your game by providing detailed information on courses, distances, and key metrics for your performance. The watch helps you make more informed decisions on the course, such as knowing the distance to the hole or tracking your shots.

How to Use Golf Mode

1. **Activate Golf Mode**:

    o To activate **Golf Mode**, open the **Samsung Health app** and scroll to the **Golf** section, or tap on the **Golf Mode** icon in the App Drawer on your Galaxy Watch5 Pro.

2. **Select a Course**:

    o The **Galaxy Watch5 Pro** comes with a database of thousands of golf courses worldwide. You can either search for your desired golf course by name or use your **location services** to automatically display nearby courses.

    o Select the course you're playing on, and the watch will load the course map with hole-by-hole details.

3. **Tracking Your Game**:

    o As you play, the **Galaxy Watch5 Pro** will track your shots, the distance to the hole, and your overall performance. The watch provides key data points such as:

- **Shot distance**: Measure the distance of each shot to improve accuracy and consistency.

- **Course maps**: View detailed maps of the course, showing distances from the tee to the green, as well as obstacles like bunkers and water hazards.

- **Hole-by-hole information**: Get live data for each hole, including the par, distance, and your current position on the course.

4. **Tracking Progress**:

   o The watch will automatically record your performance and give you detailed insights into each hole, including **total distance** played, **average shot distance**, and **score**.

Key Benefits of Golf Mode

- **Accurate Course Mapping**: The built-in course maps provide an easy-to-read guide to help you navigate each hole with confidence.

- **Shot Tracking**: Golf Mode allows you to track your shot distances and improve your game over time.

- **Real-Time Feedback**: Get immediate insights into your performance, helping you make strategic decisions while you play.

- **Better Game Strategy**: By knowing the distances to obstacles and the green, you can plan your shots more effectively and improve your score.

The **Samsung Galaxy Watch5 Pro** is truly a game-changer for outdoor enthusiasts and adventurers, offering a wealth of features designed to enhance navigation, performance tracking, and safety. Whether you're exploring new trails, tackling elevation changes, or enjoying a round of golf, the Galaxy Watch5 Pro has all the tools you need to track your journey and improve your experience.

With features like **route and turn-by-turn navigation**, **Track Back**, **altitude and elevation tracking**, and **Golf Mode**, this smartwatch is not just a fitness tracker; it's a complete outdoor companion that helps you navigate, track, and improve your outdoor activities. By using these tools, you can make the most of every adventure, stay safe, and track your progress as you explore the world around you.

CHAPTER 5
Customizing Your Galaxy Watch5 Pro

The **Samsung Galaxy Watch5 Pro** is a sophisticated smartwatch that is not only equipped with a wide range of advanced features for health tracking, fitness, and navigation, but it also offers a high level of customization, making it the perfect companion for your daily life and outdoor adventures. The ability to personalize your watch ensures that it not only fits your lifestyle but also reflects your personal style and preferences. Whether you're looking to change the watch face, organize widgets for easier access, or adjust settings for comfort and efficiency, the **Galaxy Watch5 Pro** makes it easy to tailor every aspect of the watch to suit your needs.

In this guide, we will walk you through the various ways to customize your Galaxy Watch5 Pro, from selecting watch faces to adjusting settings for notifications, sound, and more. We will also cover tips for choosing and switching out straps for comfort and style. Let's dive into each of the key customization options for your Galaxy Watch5 Pro.

1. Watch Faces: How to Change, Customize, and Download New Watch Faces

Your watch face is the first thing you see when you glance at your Galaxy Watch5 Pro, and customizing it allows you to make the watch your own. With a variety of built-in designs and the ability to download new faces from the Galaxy Store, you can adjust the style, functionality, and layout to suit your preferences.

How to Change the Watch Face

Changing your watch face is quick and simple:

1. **Swipe to the Watch Face**:

   o From the home screen, press and hold the current watch face until the customization options appear. The watch will vibrate, and you'll see a preview of other watch faces you can choose from.

2. **Browse Available Watch Faces**:

   o Scroll left or right to browse through a variety of default watch faces. You will find both analog and digital faces, with different designs ranging from minimalist to more detailed, fitness-focused layouts.

3. **Select a New Watch Face**:

   o Tap on the one you like to select it. Your new watch face will appear immediately, and you can see the changes reflected on your wrist.

4. **Customize Your Watch Face**:

   o For further customization, you can modify the elements that are displayed on the watch face, such as the background color, complications (e.g., heart rate, weather), and the style of the hands and markers (for analog faces).

Customizing Watch Face Features

1. **Changing Watch Face Elements**:

   o After selecting a watch face, tap **Customize** or **Edit** to access the available customization options. Here you can adjust various aspects of the face, including:

- **Background color**: Change the color of the background to suit your style or match your outfit.

- **Complications**: Customize the data fields or complications displayed on the watch face. For instance, you can choose to display your heart rate, weather, steps, or calendar events.

- **Watch Hand Design**: For analog watch faces, you can change the look of the hour and minute hands or set them to a digital format for clearer time reading.

2. **Changing Layouts**:

   o Some watch faces offer different layouts for complications. For example, a digital watch face might allow you to rearrange the widgets to place the time, weather, and steps in different positions. You can easily drag and drop them to your preferred layout.

3. **Use of Widgets and Additional Information**:

   o With **widgets**, you can add more detailed information to your watch face, including your daily activity summary, the time of sunrise or sunset, your sleep status, or even stock market data.

Downloading New Watch Faces

1. **Access the Galaxy Store**:

   o If you want more variety, head to the **Galaxy Store** for a vast selection of third-party watch faces.

   o From your **Galaxy Watch5 Pro**, open the **Galaxy Store** by swiping up on the home screen and selecting the **Store** icon.

2. **Browse and Download**:

   o In the store, browse through a wide selection of watch faces. You'll find options that range from sleek, minimalistic designs to detailed, data-driven watch faces with multiple complications.

o   Once you find a watch face you like, tap on it and select **Download**. The watch face will be added to your library and automatically applied.

3. **Sync with Your Watch**:

o   You can also browse the Galaxy Store via your phone, making it easier to see more options on a larger screen. Once you've downloaded the watch face on your phone, it will automatically sync with the watch through the **Galaxy Wearable** app.

2. Widgets and Quick Settings: Adding Widgets for Quick Access to Features

Widgets on the Galaxy Watch5 Pro are small, customizable apps that provide you with quick access to useful information, such as weather updates, heart rate monitoring, calendar events, and much more. Organizing your widgets efficiently ensures that you can view your most important data with a simple swipe.

How to Add Widgets

1. **Access the Widgets Screen**:

    o   On the main screen of your Galaxy Watch5 Pro, swipe **left** to access the **Widgets** screen. This is where all of your widgets are displayed.

2. **Adding a New Widget**:

    o   To add a widget, swipe down to the bottom of the screen, and select the **Add Widget** button (the plus icon).

    o   Browse through the available widget options. You can find widgets for weather, heart rate, exercise stats, calendar, alarms, and more.

    o   Select the widget you want to add, and it will be automatically placed in your widget screen.

3. **Rearranging Widgets**:

    o   To customize the order of your widgets, tap and hold the widget you want to move. After holding, drag it to the desired position in the list. Release your finger when the widget is in the correct location.

- o This allows you to prioritize the widgets you use most frequently.

4. **Remove Unused Widgets**:

- o If there are widgets you don't use or no longer need, you can remove them by selecting the widget, then tapping **Remove** or swiping it away.

Quick Settings for Fast Access

The **Quick Settings** menu provides immediate access to essential features, such as volume control, Wi-Fi settings, Do Not Disturb mode, and more.

1. **How to Access Quick Settings**:

- o Swipe **down** from the top of your screen to open the **Quick Settings** menu. Here, you can see a list of quick toggles for important features.

2. **Customizing Quick Settings**:

   o To change what appears in Quick Settings,
   open the **Settings** app on your watch, go to
   Quick Settings, and choose the options you
   want to be displayed. You can add or remove
   toggles for things like Wi-Fi, Bluetooth,
   airplane mode, brightness, and more.

3. Strap and Personalization: Tips on Selecting the Right Strap for Comfort and Style

The **strap** of your Galaxy Watch5 Pro plays a significant
role in both comfort and style. Since you'll likely wear your
watch all day, selecting the right strap is essential to ensure
it feels comfortable and complements your personal style.
Samsung offers several options, from sporty silicone straps
to luxurious leather and metal bands.

Selecting the Right Strap for Comfort

1. **Material Matters**:

   o **Silicone Straps**: These are the most common
   and are ideal for active users who engage in
   workouts or outdoor activities. They're
   lightweight, breathable, and easy to clean,
   making them great for fitness enthusiasts.

o **Leather Straps**: If you prefer a more classic, sophisticated look, leather straps are a great option. While not as breathable as silicone, leather adds a touch of elegance and can be more comfortable for everyday wear.

o **Metal Bands**: For a more premium, formal look, metal bands (such as stainless steel) offer durability and style. These are best suited for users who want a sleek, professional appearance.

2. **Choosing the Right Size**:

o **Fit and Comfort**: Ensure that the strap fits snugly around your wrist without being too tight or too loose. A comfortable fit is essential for accurate heart rate monitoring and to ensure the watch remains secure during activities.

o **Adjustable Bands**: Look for bands with adjustable lengths or clasps that allow you to change the size for a personalized fit. Many straps have holes or links that can be adjusted to your wrist's size.

3. **Switching Between Straps**:

    o The Galaxy Watch5 Pro features **quick-release pins**, allowing you to easily switch straps without the need for any tools. Simply press the button on the back of the watch to remove the strap, then attach a new one.

4. **Style Considerations**:

    o When selecting a strap, think about your personal style and the activities you'll be doing. A **sporty silicone strap** might be perfect for workouts, while a **leather band** is a great choice for meetings or dinner events. For a more luxurious touch, a **metal band** can elevate your watch's appearance.

Customizing the Look of Your Watch

In addition to selecting the right strap, you can customize your **watch face** and **widgets** to create a consistent look that matches your personal aesthetic. For example, pairing a classic leather band with a minimalist analog watch face gives off a sophisticated vibe, while a bright-colored silicone strap and an activity-focused watch face convey a sporty, dynamic look.

4. Settings Adjustments: How to Adjust Settings for Sound, Notifications, and Screen Preferences

The **Galaxy Watch5 Pro** offers numerous settings that allow you to personalize your device, including sound preferences, notification settings, and screen adjustments. These settings help you customize the watch for both comfort and functionality.

Adjusting Sound Settings

1. **Change Volume**:

    o To adjust the volume of your watch, swipe down from the home screen to open the **Quick Settings** menu. You will see a **volume icon**. Tap it to adjust the sound to your desired level.

    o Alternatively, go to **Settings** > **Sounds and Vibration** > **Volume** to adjust media, call, and notification volume separately.

2. **Sound or Vibration**:

    o To choose whether you want the watch to make a sound or vibrate, head to **Settings** > **Sounds and Vibration**. You can set the device to **vibrate only**, **sound only**, or **sound and vibrate** depending on your preference.

Adjusting Notification Settings

1. **Managing Notifications**:

   o Navigate to **Settings** > **Notifications** to customize how you receive alerts for calls, messages, apps, and reminders.

   o You can choose to receive notifications on the watch or turn them off entirely for specific apps. You can also set **Do Not Disturb** mode when you need a break from notifications.

2. **Managing App Notifications**:

   o For detailed control, open the **Galaxy Wearable app** on your smartphone, and go to **Notifications**. You can toggle specific apps to allow or block notifications, ensuring that only the most important ones reach you.

Adjusting Screen Preferences

1. **Brightness**:

   o To adjust the brightness of your screen, swipe down to access **Quick Settings**, and tap the **Brightness** icon. You can adjust it manually or select **Auto** to let the watch adjust based on ambient lighting.

   o For better battery life, consider setting the brightness to a lower level when not in direct sunlight.

2. **Always-On Display**:

   o The Galaxy Watch5 Pro features an **Always-On Display** (AOD) that allows you to see the time and essential information even when the watch is not in active use. To adjust this feature, go to **Settings** > **Display** > **Always On Display**. You can toggle it on or off or choose to display limited information, like the time and date, for minimal power usage.

3. **Screen Timeout**:

     o   If you want to save battery life, you can adjust the **screen timeout** by navigating to **Settings** > **Display** > **Screen Timeout**. You can choose a shorter timeout period, like 15 seconds, to save power when the watch is inactive.

The **Samsung Galaxy Watch5 Pro** offers unparalleled customization, allowing you to tailor every aspect of the watch to suit your preferences, style, and functional needs. From choosing and customizing your watch face to adjusting settings for sound, notifications, and screen preferences, the Galaxy Watch5 Pro ensures that your smartwatch is as unique as you are.

With easy-to-use controls for adjusting settings, switching straps, and adding widgets, you can personalize your watch to fit seamlessly into your daily routine. Whether you prefer a sleek, minimalist design or a vibrant, data-packed interface, the **Galaxy Watch5 Pro** allows you to take control of its appearance and functionality, providing both form and function in equal measure.

By following the steps in this guide, you can ensure that your Galaxy Watch5 Pro not only works for you but also looks and feels exactly how you want it, making it the perfect wearable for any occasion.

CHAPTER 6

Connecting with Other Devices and Accessories

The **Samsung Galaxy Watch5 Pro** is more than just a stylish timepiece—it's a comprehensive tool designed to make your life easier by connecting to a wide range of devices and accessories. Whether you want to listen to music wirelessly through Bluetooth headphones, make payments with **Samsung Pay**, or integrate your watch into your **smart home**, the Galaxy Watch5 Pro offers seamless connectivity options that enhance your everyday life. Additionally, the watch provides **LTE support** for users who want to stay connected even when their phone isn't nearby.

In this comprehensive guide, we will explore the various ways you can connect your **Galaxy Watch5 Pro** to other devices and accessories. From Bluetooth and Wi-Fi connectivity to using **Samsung Pay** for contactless payments, integrating with smart home devices, and using the watch independently with LTE, this guide will help you get the most out of your smartwatch.

1. Bluetooth and Wi-Fi Connectivity: Connecting the Watch to Bluetooth Devices and Wi-Fi Networks

The **Galaxy Watch5 Pro** offers robust **Bluetooth** and **Wi-Fi** connectivity, allowing you to connect your watch to various devices, such as Bluetooth headphones, speakers, and even your smartphone, to enhance its functionality.

Connecting to Bluetooth Devices (Headphones, Speakers, etc.)

1. **Activate Bluetooth on Your Galaxy Watch5 Pro**:

   o Open the **Settings** app on your Galaxy Watch5 Pro.

   o Scroll down and tap on **Connections**.

   o Tap **Bluetooth** and ensure it is turned on. Your watch will begin searching for available Bluetooth devices nearby.

2. **Pairing with Bluetooth Headphones or Speakers**:

   o While the Bluetooth settings are open on your watch, put your Bluetooth headphones or speaker into pairing mode. This usually involves holding down a button on the device (such as the power button) until a flashing light indicates it's in pairing mode.

o Your **Galaxy Watch5 Pro** will display a list of available Bluetooth devices. Tap on the name of your headphones or speakers from the list to pair the devices.

o Once paired, the watch will automatically connect to the audio device, allowing you to stream music or listen to notifications directly through the Bluetooth-connected headphones or speakers.

3. **Adjusting Audio Settings**:

o After connecting your Bluetooth device, you can adjust the volume by swiping up from the main screen to access **Quick Settings**.

o You can also adjust the volume within the **Settings** > **Sounds and Vibration** menu.

Connecting to Wi-Fi Networks

In addition to Bluetooth connectivity, the **Galaxy Watch5 Pro** supports **Wi-Fi** connectivity, which is helpful when you want to connect to the internet without using your smartphone as a hotspot.

1. **Connect to Wi-Fi:**

   o From the **Settings** menu on your watch, scroll down to **Connections** and select **Wi-Fi**.

   o Toggle **Wi-Fi** on, and the watch will start scanning for nearby Wi-Fi networks.

   o Select your Wi-Fi network from the list, and enter the **Wi-Fi password** when prompted.

2. **Use Wi-Fi for Internet Connectivity:**

   o Once connected to Wi-Fi, your Galaxy Watch5 Pro will use the network to download apps, receive notifications, and sync data without the need to have your phone nearby.

   o This feature is particularly useful when you're out and about and want to use the internet on your watch while leaving your phone at home.

3. **Managing Wi-Fi Connections**:

  o You can manage Wi-Fi networks and connections by going to **Settings** > **Connections** > **Wi-Fi**. Here, you can view connected networks and switch between networks as needed.

Using Bluetooth and Wi-Fi Simultaneously

- You can use Bluetooth and Wi-Fi simultaneously for optimal connectivity. For instance, while using **Bluetooth** headphones to listen to music, your watch can still stay connected to Wi-Fi for syncing notifications or updating apps. This makes the **Galaxy Watch5 Pro** a versatile device that keeps you connected in all situations.

2. Using NFC and Samsung Pay: Step-by-Step Instructions on How to Set Up Samsung Pay for Contactless Payments

One of the most convenient features of the **Samsung Galaxy Watch5 Pro** is its ability to make **contactless payments** using **Samsung Pay**. Whether you're grabbing a coffee or shopping at a retail store, you can make quick and secure payments directly from your watch without needing to carry your wallet or phone.

Setting Up Samsung Pay on Your Galaxy Watch5 Pro

1. **Install Samsung Pay**:

   o   Samsung Pay should already be pre-installed on your Galaxy Watch5 Pro. If it's not installed, you can download it from the **Galaxy Store** on your watch or the **Galaxy Wearable app** on your paired smartphone.

2. **Set Up Samsung Pay**:

   o   Open the **Samsung Pay** app on your watch.

   o   Follow the on-screen instructions to set up your payment methods. You'll need to add a **credit card** or **debit card** to the watch for payment processing. This process may require you to authenticate your payment details through the **Samsung Pay** app on your phone or directly on the watch.

3. **Add Cards to Samsung Pay**:

   o   To add a new card, tap on **Add Card** within the **Samsung Pay** app and enter the card details manually or use your smartphone's **camera** to scan the card.

o   Verify your card details and authenticate using a PIN or biometric authentication (e.g., fingerprint, facial recognition) for security.

4. **Set a Default Card**:

o   Once you've added multiple cards, you can set a default card by selecting the **default payment method** in the **Samsung Pay** settings. This ensures that the card you use most often is selected automatically for payments.

Making Payments with Samsung Pay

1. **Initiating a Payment**:

o   To make a payment, simply hold your wrist close to the payment terminal.

o   Open the **Samsung Pay** app on your watch, and tap the **Pay** button. You may need to enter your PIN or authenticate using **biometrics**.

2. **Payment Confirmation**:

    o Once the payment is processed, the terminal will confirm the transaction, and you will receive a **vibration** or **notification** on your watch, indicating that the payment has been completed successfully.

3. **Managing Payment Methods**:

    o You can manage your payment cards, change the default card, or delete cards directly from the **Samsung Pay** app. If you need to update or replace your card information, simply open the app and select **Settings > Cards**.

Benefits of Samsung Pay

- **Convenience**: Make fast, secure payments directly from your watch, eliminating the need for physical cards or cash.

- **Security**: Payments are secured with **tokenization** and **biometric authentication**, ensuring your card details are protected.

- **Widely Accepted**: Samsung Pay is accepted at most stores and terminals that support **NFC (Near Field**

Communication) payments, making it a convenient solution for many everyday purchases.

3. Smart Home Integration: Using Your Galaxy Watch5 Pro as Part of Your Smart Home Setup

The **Samsung Galaxy Watch5 Pro** is not just a fitness tracker; it can also serve as a **hub** for controlling your **smart home devices**. By integrating your watch with your smart home ecosystem, you can manage everything from lights to thermostats, all from your wrist.

Setting Up Smart Home Integration

1. **Linking to SmartThings**:

   o First, ensure that your smart home devices (lights, thermostats, security cameras, etc.) are compatible with **SmartThings**, Samsung's smart home platform.

   o Open the **SmartThings app** on your Galaxy Watch5 Pro or smartphone and ensure that your devices are properly set up within the app.

2. **Connecting Your Watch to SmartThings**:

   o On your watch, open the **SmartThings app** and follow the on-screen instructions to sync your **Galaxy Watch5 Pro** with your SmartThings ecosystem.

   o Once synced, the **SmartThings app** on your watch will allow you to control compatible devices, including **lights**, **thermostats**, **door locks**, and **smart plugs**.

3. **Managing Smart Home Devices**:

   o From the **SmartThings app** on your Galaxy Watch5 Pro, you can view the status of all connected devices and control them directly. For example, you can adjust the temperature of your home's thermostat, turn on or off lights, and even lock or unlock doors—all from the convenience of your wrist.

Smart Home Control Examples

1. **Adjusting Lights**:

   o With the **SmartThings app**, you can control your lights by turning them on or off, adjusting brightness, or changing the color (if your lights are RGB-enabled).

2. **Managing Temperature**:

    o   Adjust your **smart thermostat** settings, whether you want to cool down or warm up your home, directly from your wrist using the **SmartThings** app.

3. **Checking Security**:

    o   View **security cameras** or lock and unlock **smart doors** for added convenience and peace of mind.

Voice Control with Bixby:

*   You can also use **Bixby**, Samsung's virtual assistant, to control smart home devices. Simply say commands like "Hey Bixby, turn off the living room lights" or "Hey Bixby, set the thermostat to 72°F" to control your smart home hands-free.

Benefits of Smart Home Integration

*   **Convenience**: Control your home with just a tap or voice command, making it easier to manage your environment.

- **Energy Efficiency**: Adjust your thermostat and lighting to optimize energy usage, reducing unnecessary consumption.

- **Security**: Keep track of your smart home devices, ensuring your home is secure, even when you're away.

4. Using the Watch Independently with LTE: Guide to Setting Up LTE for the LTE Model

If you have the **LTE model** of the **Galaxy Watch5 Pro**, you have the added advantage of being able to use your watch independently from your phone. LTE connectivity allows you to make calls, send messages, stream music, and access apps without needing to be paired with a smartphone.

Setting Up LTE on Your Galaxy Watch5 Pro

1. **Activate LTE Service**:

   o Ensure that you have an active **mobile plan** that supports **LTE** for your Galaxy Watch5 Pro. This often involves adding a wearable plan through your mobile carrier.

   o Open the **Galaxy Wearable app** on your phone and select **Mobile Plans**. Choose **Add**

Plan and follow the instructions to activate the LTE service for your watch.

2. **Setting Up eSIM**:

   o   Your Galaxy Watch5 Pro uses an **eSIM** (embedded SIM) to connect to the LTE network. Your carrier will provide an eSIM profile to activate on the watch.

   o   Once the eSIM is activated, your watch will be able to use mobile data for calling, texting, and internet access, independent of your phone.

3. **Testing LTE Connectivity**:

   o   Once set up, turn off your phone and test the LTE functionality on your watch. Try making a call, sending a message, or streaming music without your phone nearby to ensure everything is working properly.

Using LTE for Communication and Entertainment

1. **Making Calls**:

   o   With LTE enabled, you can make and receive calls directly from the watch without needing to carry your phone. Use the **Contacts app** to dial numbers or answer incoming calls through the watch's microphone and speaker.

2. **Sending Messages**:

   o You can send **SMS messages** or use apps like **WhatsApp** or **Facebook Messenger** to stay connected with friends and family while you're on the go.

3. **Streaming Music and Podcasts**:

   o Use **Spotify** or **YouTube Music** to stream your favorite tunes or podcasts directly to Bluetooth headphones connected to your watch, even without your phone.

Benefits of Using LTE with Your Galaxy Watch5 Pro

- **Independence**: You can leave your phone at home or in your bag and still stay connected for calls, messages, and apps.

- **Convenience**: Ideal for outdoor activities like running or hiking, where carrying your phone isn't ideal, yet you still need connectivity for safety or entertainment.

- **Streamlining**: LTE functionality allows you to streamline your activities by reducing the need to switch between devices.

The **Samsung Galaxy Watch5 Pro** offers a remarkable array of connectivity features, making it much more than just a fitness tracker or smartwatch. Whether you're looking to connect to Bluetooth devices like headphones, make secure payments using **Samsung Pay**, control your **smart home devices**, or use **LTE** for independent communication, the **Galaxy Watch5 Pro** has everything you need to stay connected, productive, and entertained, all from your wrist.

By following the steps outlined in this guide, you can fully unlock the potential of your **Galaxy Watch5 Pro** and integrate it seamlessly into your lifestyle. With its advanced connectivity features, this smartwatch offers unmatched versatility, ensuring that you're always connected and ready for whatever life throws your way.

CHAPTER 7

Maintaining Your Galaxy Watch5 Pro

The **Samsung Galaxy Watch5 Pro** is a sophisticated and versatile smartwatch packed with advanced features that cater to fitness, connectivity, and daily convenience. To ensure that your watch remains in optimal condition and functions seamlessly over time, it's important to follow proper maintenance practices. This includes managing battery life, charging the watch correctly, cleaning it regularly, and troubleshooting common issues.

In this comprehensive guide, we will cover everything you need to know about maintaining your **Galaxy Watch5 Pro**. From battery management tips to cleaning and troubleshooting common issues, this guide will help you keep your watch running smoothly for the long haul.

1. Battery Management: Tips on Extending Battery Life

One of the most important factors for ensuring your **Galaxy Watch5 Pro** performs at its best is effective **battery management**. While the watch is equipped with a powerful battery, there are several strategies you can implement to optimize power consumption and make the most out of each charge.

Tips for Extending Battery Life

1. **Enable Power Saving Mode**:

    o   The **Galaxy Watch5 Pro** features a **Power Saving Mode** that reduces power consumption by turning off non-essential features, such as the always-on display and background app updates. To activate **Power Saving Mode**:

        ▪   Open the **Settings** app on your watch.

        ▪   Go to **Battery** and select **Power Saving Mode**.

        ▪   You can choose to enable it immediately or set a schedule for it to activate automatically.

    o   When Power Saving Mode is enabled, your watch will display only essential information, helping you extend battery life for a longer period.

2. **Turn Off Always-On Display**:

   o The **Always-On Display (AOD)** feature is convenient, but it can drain your battery if left on all the time. Turning it off can help improve battery longevity. To disable AOD:

      ▪ Go to **Settings** > **Display** > **Always On Display**.

      ▪ Toggle off the option to disable this feature. You can manually turn it on when needed.

3. **Manage Notifications**:

   o Constant notifications can cause your watch to consume unnecessary power as it continuously checks for updates. You can reduce power consumption by limiting the number of apps that send notifications. To manage notifications:

      ▪ Go to **Settings** > **Notifications**.

      ▪ Choose which apps can send you notifications and mute unnecessary ones.

- Consider enabling **Do Not Disturb** during times when you don't need to be disturbed, such as during workouts or sleep.

4. **Disable Background Apps**:

   o Some apps on your **Galaxy Watch5 Pro** run in the background, consuming energy even when you're not actively using them. To optimize battery life, you can disable background apps:

      - Open the **Samsung Health app** or any app running in the background.

      - Close apps you aren't actively using by swiping up from the home screen to access the **App Drawer** and selecting **Close All**.

5. **Limit GPS Use**:

   o GPS is a feature that can quickly drain the battery, especially during long outdoor activities such as hiking, running, or cycling. To preserve battery while using GPS, limit its use by only turning on GPS when necessary:

- If you're using the **Galaxy Watch5 Pro** for running or cycling, use **GPS only when needed** for tracking distance or location.

- If you don't need GPS for your activity, switch to **Indoor Running** or **Cycling** modes, which do not require GPS.

6. **Reduce Screen Brightness**:

   o Reducing the brightness of your watch's screen can significantly help conserve battery. To adjust the brightness:

   - Go to **Settings** > **Display** > **Brightness**.

   - Adjust the brightness to a level that's comfortable for you without unnecessarily draining the battery.

7. **Use Energy-Saving Apps**:

   o Some apps are designed to be more energy-efficient, reducing battery consumption without sacrificing functionality. Look for energy-saving modes in apps like **Spotify** or **Samsung Health**, which can help minimize battery drain during extended use.

When to Charge the Watch

1. **Avoid Full Discharges**: Try to keep the watch's battery between 20% and 80% for optimal longevity. Frequent full discharges and charges can shorten the battery's lifespan over time.

2. **Charge Regularly**: Charging your Galaxy Watch5 Pro every night (or whenever you're not using it) can help maintain its battery health and ensure that you're always ready to use it.

2. Charging the Watch: Instructions on How to Properly Charge the Galaxy Watch5 Pro

Charging your **Galaxy Watch5 Pro** correctly ensures the longevity of both the battery and the overall performance of the device. The watch comes with a **magnetic charging dock** that makes charging quick and easy.

How to Properly Charge Your Galaxy Watch5 Pro

1. **Use the Included Charger**:

   o The **Galaxy Watch5 Pro** comes with a **magnetic charging dock** and USB-C cable. For best results, always use the provided charging equipment to ensure proper charging speeds and safety.

   o The magnetic charging dock allows you to easily snap your watch into place without worrying about aligning charging pins. Simply place the back of the watch onto the magnetic charger, ensuring it is securely attached.

2. **Ensure Proper Placement**:

   o Place the watch onto the charging dock with the back of the watch facing down. The charging dock will attach magnetically, and you should feel it snap into place.

   o Double-check that the charging pins on the watch align with the corresponding pins on the charger. If your watch is not charging, gently reposition it to ensure proper contact.

3. **Charging Time**:

   o The **Galaxy Watch5 Pro** charges relatively quickly, typically reaching **50% charge in about 30 minutes** and **fully charging in under 90 minutes**. You'll see the **charging indicator** on the watch screen as the battery fills up.

4. **Charging via Wireless Charging Pad**:

   o The **Galaxy Watch5 Pro** is also compatible with any **Qi-enabled wireless charging pad**, which means you can charge it using wireless charging stations.

   o To charge the watch with a wireless pad, simply place the back of the watch on the pad, aligning it as you would with the included charging dock. Make sure the pad is connected to a power source.

Best Practices for Charging

1. **Avoid Overcharging**: The **Galaxy Watch5 Pro** has built-in protection that prevents overcharging, but it's still a good practice not to leave your watch on the charger for extended periods once it reaches 100%.

110

This helps maintain the health of the battery in the long term.

2. **Charge Regularly**: It's recommended to charge your **Galaxy Watch5 Pro** nightly or when the battery reaches around 20%, so you don't risk running out of power during the day.

3. **Avoid Charging While It's Hot**: If your watch is too hot (e.g., after a workout), avoid charging it until it cools down to prevent potential heat damage to the battery.

3. Cleaning and Care: Best Practices for Cleaning the Watch, Including the Strap and Display

To ensure the longevity and aesthetic appeal of your **Galaxy Watch5 Pro**, regular cleaning and maintenance are essential. Keeping your watch clean not only enhances its appearance but also helps maintain the functionality of the display and sensors.

How to Clean the Watch and Strap

1. **Cleaning the Watch Display**:

    o Use a **microfiber cloth** to gently wipe the watch display. This will remove fingerprints, dust, and smudges without scratching the screen.

o For stubborn marks or dirt, lightly dampen the cloth with **water** or a **screen-safe cleaner**. Avoid using harsh chemicals or abrasive materials, as these can damage the watch's display or the coating.

o For extra care, you can use a **soft-bristle brush** to remove any dirt from the edges of the screen.

2. **Cleaning the Strap**:

o **Silicone Straps**: To clean the silicone strap, simply rinse it with **warm water** and **mild soap**. Avoid using strong detergents or chemicals that can cause the material to break down. After cleaning, dry the strap thoroughly with a clean towel.

o **Leather Straps**: Leather straps should be cleaned with a soft, dry cloth to remove dirt and moisture. If needed, you can use a **leather conditioner** to maintain the leather's softness and prevent cracking. Avoid soaking leather straps in water.

- o **Metal Bands**: For **metal** bands, use a **soft cloth** to polish the surface. A **mild metal cleaner** can be used if needed, but make sure it's safe for your watch's material.

3. **Cleaning the Sensors**:

- o The back of your **Galaxy Watch5 Pro** contains sensors that monitor heart rate, blood oxygen, and other fitness metrics. To ensure accurate readings, keep the sensors clean. Use a dry **microfiber cloth** or a **soft brush** to remove any dust, dirt, or oils that may build up on the back of the watch.

4. **Avoiding Water Damage**:

- o The **Galaxy Watch5 Pro** is **5ATM water-resistant**, meaning it can handle exposure to water, such as during swimming or rainy weather. However, it's important to clean your watch after exposure to water, especially if you've been in saltwater or chlorine. Rinse the watch with fresh water to prevent any build-up of residue or damage.

Maintaining the Strap's Durability

- **Check the Strap Regularly**: Over time, the strap may stretch, loosen, or show signs of wear. Inspect your strap regularly to ensure it is still secure and in good condition. If it appears to be damaged or worn out, consider replacing it with a new strap.

- **Avoid Extreme Conditions**: Keep the watch and strap away from extreme heat or cold, which could cause materials to warp or break down. If you're engaged in activities that might cause excessive wear (like heavy lifting), switch to a more durable strap, such as a leather or metal option.

4. Troubleshooting Common Issues: Solutions for Connectivity Problems, Syncing Errors, and Display Glitches

Despite its advanced technology, you may encounter occasional issues with your **Galaxy Watch5 Pro**. Whether you're having trouble with **connectivity**, experiencing **syncing errors**, or noticing glitches in the display, this section will guide you through some common troubleshooting solutions.

1. Connectivity Problems

If your Galaxy Watch5 Pro is having trouble connecting to your phone, Wi-Fi, or Bluetooth devices, try the following steps:

1. **Bluetooth Connectivity Issues**:

    o Ensure that **Bluetooth** is enabled on both your watch and the paired device (such as your smartphone or headphones).

    o If the watch isn't connecting to your phone, try **disconnecting** and **re-pairing** the devices:

        ▪ Go to **Settings** > **Connections** > **Bluetooth**, and select the device you want to reconnect to. Tap **Forget** and then try pairing again.

    o If pairing issues persist, restart both the watch and the phone to reset the connection.

2. **Wi-Fi Issues**:

   o Make sure that your watch is within range of the Wi-Fi network.

   o Try turning **Wi-Fi** off and on again, or disconnect and reconnect to the network from the **Settings** > **Connections** > **Wi-Fi** menu.

3. **Syncing Errors with Samsung Health**:

   o If your watch isn't syncing data with the **Samsung Health app**, ensure that both the watch and phone are connected and that **Bluetooth** is on.

   o Try **force-quitting** the app on your phone and restarting both devices. Then, open the **Samsung Health app** and check if the sync is successful.

   o You can also try **logging out and back into your Samsung account**.

2. Display Glitches

If you notice glitches or problems with the display, such as unresponsive touch or flickering:

1. **Restart the Watch**:

   o Press and hold the **power button** to restart the watch. This will help clear any temporary software glitches.

2. **Reset the Watch**:

   o If issues persist, consider performing a **factory reset**:

     ▪ Go to **Settings** > **General** > **Reset**.

     ▪ This will erase all data on the watch, so make sure to back up any important information before resetting.

Maintaining your **Samsung Galaxy Watch5 Pro** is essential to ensuring it continues to perform at its best. By managing battery life, charging the device properly, cleaning it regularly, and troubleshooting common issues, you can maximize its lifespan and keep it functioning seamlessly.

Following the tips in this guide will help you optimize your watch's performance, ensure comfort, and address any problems you might encounter. Whether it's extending battery life, keeping the display clean, or fixing syncing errors, these maintenance practices will ensure that your **Galaxy Watch5 Pro** remains a reliable companion for all your daily tasks and fitness activities.

CHAPTER 8

Exploring Additional Features of the Samsung Galaxy Watch5 Pro

The **Samsung Galaxy Watch5 Pro** is designed to be more than just a smartwatch for fitness tracking. It's a versatile device that integrates seamlessly into daily life, offering a variety of features designed to make everything—from communication and entertainment to productivity and health management—easier and more efficient. In this guide, we will explore the additional features of the **Galaxy Watch5 Pro**, including **music and media playback**, **notifications and alerts**, **voice commands with Bixby**, and **smart notifications**. Understanding how to make the most of these features will help you unlock the full potential of your watch.

1. Music and Media Playback: How to Store Music on the Watch or Connect It to a Music Streaming Service

Music is an essential part of many people's lives, and the **Samsung Galaxy Watch5 Pro** makes it easier than ever to listen to your favorite tunes directly from your wrist. Whether you're out for a run, working out, or simply relaxing, you can enjoy music and media playback through your watch, even without needing to keep your phone nearby.

Storing Music on the Watch

1. **Using the Music App**:

    o The **Samsung Galaxy Watch5 Pro** comes with a built-in **Music** app that allows you to store and play music directly from the watch. This is especially helpful when you want to leave your phone at home but still enjoy your music while on the go.

2. **Adding Music to Your Watch**:

    o First, ensure that your watch is connected to your **Samsung Galaxy Wearable app** on your phone.

    o Open the **Music** app on your watch.

    o From the **Samsung Galaxy Wearable app**, tap on **Add Content to Your Watch**. Here you can select music files to sync from your phone to your watch. This can include tracks from your **local music library**, **Spotify**, or

YouTube Music if you have subscriptions or offline downloads.

- o Choose your favorite playlists or albums to add to the watch. Depending on the amount of music, this may take a few minutes to transfer.

3. **Listening to Music on Your Watch**:

- o Once your music is stored, open the **Music app** on the watch to browse your tracks, albums, or playlists.

- o Pair your **Bluetooth headphones** or **speakers** with the watch, and you'll be able to listen to your music directly from the Galaxy Watch5 Pro.

Connecting the Watch to a Music Streaming Service

For those who prefer streaming music from popular services like **Spotify**, **Apple Music**, or **YouTube Music**, the **Galaxy Watch5 Pro** supports direct integration with these platforms.

1. **Spotify Integration**:

   o To use **Spotify** on your watch, ensure you have the **Spotify app** installed on both your phone and the watch. Open the **Galaxy Store** and download the app if it's not already installed.

   o Once installed, log in to your **Spotify account** on the watch. You can now browse your playlists, discover new tracks, and stream music directly from the watch. You can also control playback from the watch, including skipping songs, adjusting volume, and even downloading music for offline use.

2. **Other Streaming Services**:

   o The **Galaxy Watch5 Pro** supports additional music streaming apps, including **YouTube Music** and **Deezer**, via the **Samsung Galaxy Wearable app**.

   o For apps like **Apple Music**, users can connect their accounts through third-party apps or sync downloaded content to their watch for offline listening.

3. **Using the Watch Without the Phone**:

   o One of the greatest advantages of storing music on the **Galaxy Watch5 Pro** is the ability to listen to music without needing your phone. Whether you're running or cycling, simply connect your Bluetooth headphones to the watch, and you're ready to go.

Managing Media Playback

- The **Galaxy Watch5 Pro** allows you to control music playback directly from the watch. You can pause, play, skip songs, and adjust the volume without touching your phone.

- Use the **Now Playing** feature to see the title of the current song and artist, along with album art. You can also add music to a playlist directly from the watch.

2. Notifications and Alerts: How to Set Up and Manage Notifications for Calls, Messages, and App Alerts

One of the key features of a smartwatch is its ability to manage notifications and alerts, ensuring that you never miss an important call, message, or reminder. The **Samsung**

Galaxy Watch5 Pro is designed to provide efficient notification management, allowing you to stay connected and in control.

Setting Up Notifications for Calls and Messages

1. **Enabling Call and Message Alerts**:

   o On your **Galaxy Watch5 Pro**, go to **Settings** > **Notifications** > **App Notifications**.

   o Enable **calls and messages** notifications by toggling them on. This allows the watch to notify you when you receive incoming calls, messages, or app notifications.

   o You can choose whether you want to receive alerts for specific apps or all apps. Select the apps you want to be notified about, including messaging apps like **WhatsApp**, **SMS**, **Facebook Messenger**, and more.

2. **Responding to Notifications**:

   o When a call or message comes in, your watch will vibrate and display the alert. You can answer calls directly from the watch or reject them with a swipe.

o   For text messages, you can either read the message directly on the watch or reply using quick replies, voice-to-text, or the on-screen keyboard. Depending on the app, you may also have the option to send emojis or preset responses.

3. **Managing Notification Sounds and Vibration**:

o   Customize your notification preferences under **Settings** > **Sounds and Vibration**. You can choose from various notification sounds or enable vibration mode for silent alerts.

o   If you need to stay undisturbed, you can activate **Do Not Disturb** mode, which silences all notifications for a designated period.

Managing App Alerts

1. **Customizing App Notifications**:

o   Go to **Settings** > **Notifications** > **App Notifications**, where you can control which apps send you alerts.

o You can choose to enable or disable notifications for each app, giving you complete control over what you receive. For example, you may want to keep notifications on for calendar events and fitness reminders but turn off non-essential notifications from games or news apps.

2. **Setting Priorities for Notifications**:

o To prioritize certain alerts, you can enable **Priority Mode** under **Settings** > **Notifications**. This ensures that only the most important notifications, such as calls and texts, will come through when your watch is on priority mode.

3. **Using Smart Notifications**:

o The **Galaxy Watch5 Pro** allows you to set **Smart Notifications**, which display important information based on your location or activity. For example, you can receive weather updates based your location, calendar reminders when you're on the go, or

126

fitness alerts when you've been inactive for too long.

3. Voice Commands with Bixby: Using Samsung's Voice Assistant to Control the Watch Hands-Free

Bixby, Samsung's intelligent voice assistant, is built directly into the **Galaxy Watch5 Pro**, allowing you to control your watch and access features hands-free. Whether you want to start a workout, check the weather, or send a message, Bixby can assist you with voice commands.

Activating Bixby

1. **Using Bixby on Your Watch**:

   o To activate **Bixby**, press and hold the **Home button** (the lower button) until the voice assistant pops up. Alternatively, you can say **"Hey Bixby"** to trigger the assistant hands-free.

2. **Giving Commands**:

   o After activating Bixby, you can issue a wide range of commands. For example:

- "Hey Bixby, start a workout."

- "Hey Bixby, set a timer for 10 minutes."

- "Hey Bixby, send a message to John."

o Bixby will respond by performing the action or providing the information you requested.

3. **Voice Feedback**:

o Bixby offers voice feedback, so you can hear responses and confirmations for commands you give. This allows for hands-free operation, perfect when you're working out or in a situation where using your hands isn't ideal.

Common Bixby Commands

1. **Fitness and Health**:

o **"Hey Bixby, start a run."**

o **"Hey Bixby, check my heart rate."**

o **"Hey Bixby, track my sleep."**

2. **General Requests**:

   o "Hey Bixby, what's the weather today?"

   o "Hey Bixby, set an alarm for 7 AM."

   o "Hey Bixby, turn off Do Not Disturb."

3. **Smart Home Control**:

   o "Hey Bixby, turn on the living room lights."

   o "Hey Bixby, adjust the thermostat to 72 degrees."

Controlling Third-Party Apps with Bixby

In addition to controlling native Samsung apps, **Bixby** can also interact with third-party apps installed on your Galaxy Watch5 Pro. For instance:

- "Hey Bixby, play music on Spotify."

- "Hey Bixby, check my messages on WhatsApp."

4. Smart Notifications: Setting Up Your Watch to Receive Important Notifications

Smart notifications are an essential feature of the **Galaxy Watch5 Pro**, allowing you to stay on top of important events and reminders throughout your day. These notifications can include everything from health reminders and weather updates to calendar events and news alerts. By customizing your smart notifications, you can ensure that you never miss crucial information while reducing unnecessary distractions.

Setting Up Calendar Reminders and Alerts

1. **Adding Calendar Events**:

   o You can sync your Google or Samsung calendar with your Galaxy Watch5 Pro, ensuring that you never miss an appointment or meeting.

   o Open the **Samsung Calendar app** or your **Google Calendar** and add events. These events will automatically sync with your watch, and you'll receive a notification on the day of the event.

2. **Customizing Event Notifications**:

   o Customize how and when you receive reminders for your calendar events. You can set a reminder to notify you a few minutes, hours, or even days before the event. To adjust this:

- Go to **Settings** > **Notifications** > **Calendar** and choose your preferences for alerts.

Weather and Location-Based Alerts

1. **Weather Notifications**:

   - The **Galaxy Watch5 Pro** can send you weather updates based on your location, keeping you informed of weather changes while you're out and about.

   - Open the **Samsung Weather app** on your watch and enable **notifications** for daily weather updates or severe weather alerts.

2. **Location-Based Reminders**:

   - You can also set location-based reminders that notify you when you reach specific places. For instance:

     - **"Hey Bixby, remind me to buy groceries when I get to the store."**

     - **"Hey Bixby, remind me to call John when I get home."**

131

Health and Fitness Reminders

1. **Activity Reminders**:

   o The **Galaxy Watch5 Pro** can send health reminders to keep you on track with your fitness goals. For instance, you can set reminders to stand up if you've been sitting for too long, or to drink water regularly throughout the day.

   o To set these reminders, go to **Settings** > **Notifications** > **Activity Reminders** and adjust the settings as per your preference.

2. **Health Tracking Alerts**:

   o The watch will also alert you if it detects abnormal heart rates or other health concerns. For example, if your heart rate exceeds a certain threshold, you'll receive a notification prompting you to check in with a healthcare provider.

   o The **Samsung Galaxy Watch5 Pro** offers a wide range of features designed to enhance your daily life through seamless connectivity and intelligent notifications. From storing and streaming music to managing notifications, controlling your smart home, and using voice commands with **Bixby**, this smartwatch ensures that you're always connected, informed, and in control.

By understanding how to optimize your music playback, notification settings, and voice commands, you can create a personalized, efficient experience that suits your needs. Whether you're on the go, working out, or simply managing your daily tasks, the **Galaxy Watch5 Pro** empowers you to stay connected and make the most of every moment.

CHAPTER 9

Troubleshooting, Updates, and Frequently Asked Questions for the Samsung Galaxy Watch5 Pro

The **Samsung Galaxy Watch5 Pro** is a highly advanced, feature-rich smartwatch, designed to offer users a seamless and integrated experience for managing fitness, notifications, communication, and entertainment. However, like any sophisticated technology, occasional issues can arise. Whether you're facing syncing problems, trying to figure out how to update the software, or dealing with a device glitch, it's important to know how to troubleshoot and resolve issues efficiently.

This guide will cover how to keep your **Galaxy Watch5 Pro** up-to-date, troubleshoot common issues, and answer some of the frequently asked questions (FAQs). We will also address customer support resources and warranty claims to help you take full advantage of the support available.

1. Software Updates: How to Update the Software of Your Galaxy Watch5 Pro for New Features and Performance Improvements

Regular **software updates** are crucial for maintaining the **Samsung Galaxy Watch5 Pro**'s performance and security. These updates bring **new features**, **performance improvements**, **bug fixes**, and ensure that your device continues to work smoothly. It's important to keep your watch updated to take full advantage of the latest enhancements.

How to Check for and Install Software Updates

1. **Ensure Your Watch is Connected to Your Phone**:

    o   Before checking for updates, ensure that your **Galaxy Watch5 Pro** is paired with your phone via the **Samsung Galaxy Wearable app**. Software updates typically require an internet connection and syncing with the phone.

2. **Open Settings on Your Watch**:

    o   On your **Galaxy Watch5 Pro**, swipe up from the home screen to access the **App Drawer**. Tap on **Settings**.

3. **Check for Updates**:

   o In **Settings**, scroll down and select **General > Software Update**.

   o Tap **Download and Install** to check for any available updates. If a new update is available, you will be prompted to download and install it.

   o Ensure that your watch is connected to a stable Wi-Fi network (or LTE if using the LTE model) for the best results.

4. **Start the Update Process**:

   o If an update is available, tap **Download**. The watch will begin downloading the update. Once the download is complete, the watch will automatically begin installing the update.

   o This process may take several minutes, depending on the size of the update and your internet speed. The watch will reboot once the installation is complete.

5. **Check for New Features**:

   o After the update is installed, you may be prompted to restart your watch. Once restarted, the new features and improvements will be ready for use.

   o To check if new features have been added, refer to the **Samsung Wearable app** or the **Samsung website** for release notes.

Automatic Updates

- **Enable Automatic Updates**: You can set your **Galaxy Watch5 Pro** to automatically download and install software updates when they become available. To enable this:

   o Go to **Settings** > **General** > **Software Update** > **Auto Update** and toggle it on.

   o This ensures that your watch always has the latest software, saving you from having to manually check for updates.

What to Do If the Update Fails

- If the software update fails to install, check the following:

- o **Connection Issues**: Ensure the watch is connected to Wi-Fi and the phone has an active internet connection.

- o **Storage Space**: If your watch has insufficient storage space, clear up some space by removing unused apps or media files.

- o **Restart Devices**: Try restarting both the **Galaxy Watch5 Pro** and the **phone** before attempting the update again.

2. Fixing Syncing Problems: Step-by-Step Instructions on How to Resolve Syncing Issues Between the Watch and Your Phone

Syncing issues between the **Galaxy Watch5 Pro** and your phone can happen for a variety of reasons, such as Bluetooth connectivity problems, account syncing issues, or software glitches. Fortunately, resolving these issues is often straightforward.

How to Fix Syncing Problems Between Your Watch and Phone

1. **Ensure Bluetooth is Enabled**:

   o The most common cause of syncing issues is a **Bluetooth connection problem**. Make sure that Bluetooth is enabled on both the **Galaxy Watch5 Pro** and your phone.

   o On your phone, open **Settings** > **Bluetooth** and ensure Bluetooth is turned on. Check if the **Galaxy Watch5 Pro** is listed as a paired device.

   o On your watch, swipe up from the home screen to open the **App Drawer**. Tap **Settings** > **Connections** and make sure Bluetooth is toggled on.

2. **Restart Both Devices**:

   o Restart both your phone and the **Galaxy Watch5 Pro** to refresh the connection. This simple step can often resolve minor connectivity issues.

3. **Re-pair the Devices**:

   o If restarting doesn't work, unpair your watch and phone and then re-pair them:

     ▪ Open the **Galaxy Wearable app** on your phone and go to **Settings** > **Connect to a new device**.

     ▪ Follow the on-screen instructions to re-pair the devices. Make sure to confirm the connection on both your phone and the watch.

4. **Ensure the Galaxy Wearable App is Updated**:

   o Outdated versions of the **Samsung Galaxy Wearable app** can cause syncing issues. Open the **Google Play Store** or **Samsung Galaxy Store**, search for **Galaxy Wearable**, and update the app if an update is available.

5. **Clear Cache and Data**:

   o If syncing problems persist, clearing the cache and data of the **Galaxy Wearable app** might help:

     ▪ On your phone, go to **Settings** > **Apps** > **Galaxy Wearable** > **Storage** > **Clear Cache**.

     ▪ Tap **Clear Data** if the problem persists (note that this will log you out of the app, and you will need to log back in).

6. **Check for App Permissions**:

   o Ensure that the **Galaxy Wearable app** has all necessary permissions enabled on your phone, including access to Bluetooth, location, and storage.

     ▪ Go to **Settings** > **Apps** > **Galaxy Wearable** > **Permissions** and ensure all relevant permissions are turned on.

7. **Syncing Health Data**:

- o If you're having trouble syncing **health data** (like steps, heart rate, or sleep data), ensure that **Samsung Health** is up to date and properly connected to the **Galaxy Wearable app**.

- o Open the **Samsung Health** app, go to **Settings**, and check if your watch is listed as a synced device.

What to Do if Syncing Continues to Fail

- **Factory Reset**: As a last resort, you can perform a factory reset on your **Galaxy Watch5 Pro**. Keep in mind that this will erase all data on the watch, so be sure to back up important data first.

  - o To reset, go to **Settings** > **General** > **Reset**.

3. Frequently Asked Questions (FAQs)

Here is a collection of frequently asked questions that can help resolve common issues or provide more clarity on using the **Samsung Galaxy Watch5 Pro**.

Q1: How do I reset my Galaxy Watch5 Pro?

1. **Factory Reset Instructions**:

   o   Open **Settings** on your watch.

   o   Scroll down to **General** > **Reset**.

   o   Tap **Factory Reset** and confirm your choice.

   o   Your watch will restart, and all data will be erased.

2. **Soft Reset**:

   o   If you just need to restart the watch without losing data, press and hold the **Power button** for 10 seconds to force a restart.

Q2: How do I sync my workouts to my phone?

1. **Syncing Health Data**:

   o   Open the **Samsung Health app** on your phone and the **Galaxy Wearable app** on your watch.

   o   Ensure that the devices are paired and connected.

- o Workouts will automatically sync between the watch and the **Samsung Health app**. If syncing fails, check Bluetooth connectivity and ensure both devices are connected to the same Wi-Fi network.

Q3: My Galaxy Watch5 Pro is not charging. What do I do?

1. **Check the Charger**:
   - o Make sure the charging dock is connected to a power source and is properly aligned with the watch's charging pins.

2. **Try Another Charger**:
   - o If the charging dock isn't working, try using a different charging cable or wireless charger that's compatible with the **Galaxy Watch5 Pro**.

3. **Restart the Watch**:
   - o Try restarting the watch before charging, as this can sometimes fix minor charging issues.

Q4: How do I enable LTE on my Galaxy Watch5 Pro?

1. **Activating LTE**:

   o Open the **Galaxy Wearable app** on your phone.

   o Go to **Mobile Plans** and follow the instructions to activate LTE service with your carrier.

   o Once activated, you can use LTE independently from your phone for calls, messages, and internet access.

Q5: How do I use Bixby on the Galaxy Watch5 Pro?

1. **Activating Bixby**:

   o Press and hold the **Home button** on your watch, or say **"Hey Bixby"** to activate the voice assistant.

   o Use Bixby to perform various tasks like setting alarms, starting workouts, controlling music, and more.

4. Customer Support and Warranty: Where to Get Help if Something Goes Wrong with Your Watch

If you're experiencing issues with your **Galaxy Watch5 Pro** that you can't resolve through troubleshooting, Samsung offers comprehensive customer support and warranty services.

Customer Support

1. **Samsung Customer Support Website**:

   o Visit the official **Samsung support website** (www.samsung.com/support) for troubleshooting guides, FAQs, and the option to chat with a Samsung representative.

2. **Samsung Customer Support App**:

   o Download the **Samsung Members app** from the **Galaxy Store** or **Google Play Store**. This app provides easy access to customer support, device diagnostics, and community forums.

3. **Phone Support**:

   o Contact Samsung's customer support by calling their dedicated support hotline. You can find the phone number for your region on the Samsung website.

Warranty and Repair

1. **Warranty Coverage**:

   o The **Samsung Galaxy Watch5 Pro** comes with a **1-year limited warranty** that covers manufacturing defects. Warranty coverage excludes damage caused by accidents, misuse, or unauthorized repairs.

2. **Repair Services**:

   o If your watch requires repair, you can either take it to an authorized Samsung service center or ship it to a repair facility. Visit the Samsung website for more information on authorized service providers in your area.

3. **Replacement and Returns**:

   o If your watch is still under warranty and is found to have a defect, Samsung may offer a replacement. If you purchased the watch recently, you may also be eligible for a return or exchange through the retailer.

The **Samsung Galaxy Watch5 Pro** is a powerful and feature-packed device that can elevate your day-to-day life through seamless integration with various apps, fitness tracking, and smart functionalities. Keeping your watch updated, troubleshooting common issues, and understanding how to use the support and warranty services available will ensure that your experience with the device remains smooth and enjoyable.

By following the steps outlined in this guide, you can maximize the use of your **Galaxy Watch5 Pro**, ensuring it continues to provide you with all the benefits it has to offer for fitness, communication, and productivity. Whether it's updating the software, resolving syncing problems, or reaching out to customer support when necessary, knowing how to manage your watch will help you maintain a high-performing, long-lasting device.

CONCLUSION

Maximizing Your Samsung Galaxy Watch5 Pro Experience: Conclusion

As we draw this guide to a close, it's important to take a step back and reflect on the many capabilities of the **Samsung Galaxy Watch5 Pro**. From its advanced health tracking features to its seamless integration with your daily life, this smartwatch has proven to be a versatile and indispensable tool that elevates the way we experience both the mundane and extraordinary moments in life. Whether you're using it to monitor your fitness goals, stay connected with loved ones, or enhance your outdoor adventures, the **Galaxy Watch5 Pro** is a device that truly adapts to your lifestyle.

Throughout this guide, you've learned how to set up your **Galaxy Watch5 Pro**, customize it to fit your personal preferences, and explore a wealth of advanced features. You've discovered how to troubleshoot common problems and maximize the use of the watch's software and hardware. By now, you're equipped to get the most out of this cutting-edge wearable, empowering you to stay on top of your health, manage your daily tasks, and experience new adventures with confidence.

The **Samsung Galaxy Watch5 Pro** isn't just a fitness tracker or a smartwatch. It's a personal companion, a tool for self-improvement, and a gateway to a more connected, healthier, and active lifestyle. Let's take a moment to recap the key benefits and features of this device, and explore how you can continue to maximize your experience with the **Galaxy Watch5 Pro** as you move forward.

Empowering Your Health and Fitness Goals

One of the most impressive aspects of the **Galaxy Watch5 Pro** is its ability to provide detailed and accurate insights into your **health and fitness**. The watch is not just a tracker; it's a **personal health assistant** that offers continuous monitoring of your vital statistics, from **heart rate** and **blood oxygen levels** to **sleep patterns** and **body composition**.

Health Monitoring

By utilizing advanced sensors, the **Galaxy Watch5 Pro** provides a deep dive into your physical well-being, allowing you to monitor real-time data on your heart rate, oxygen saturation, stress levels, and even sleep quality. These features help you make informed decisions about your health and wellness. Whether you're in a meeting, exercising, or getting ready for bed, the **Galaxy Watch5 Pro** quietly collects data, giving you a comprehensive view of your health.

Fitness Tracking

For fitness enthusiasts, the **Galaxy Watch5 Pro** offers a robust suite of tracking tools that cater to all types of workouts. From running and cycling to swimming and hiking, the **Galaxy Watch5 Pro** allows you to monitor your progress, set goals, and stay motivated. Its built-in **GPS**, **altimeter**, and **barometer** make it a perfect companion for those who love outdoor activities, while the watch's ability to track steps, calories, and distance allows you to track your progress during more routine exercises.

With these fitness features, you're not just tracking steps or calories—you're understanding the data that drives your overall health and performance. This deeper level of insight helps you set more targeted goals, track improvements, and take your fitness journey to the next level.

Staying Connected and Productive

The **Samsung Galaxy Watch5 Pro** keeps you connected with the world around you, whether you're on the go or at home. Through its integration with **Samsung's ecosystem** and **third-party apps**, the watch lets you manage notifications, receive calls, and stay on top of your calendar—all from your wrist.

Seamless Connectivity

With **Bluetooth**, **Wi-Fi**, and **LTE** support, the **Galaxy Watch5 Pro** allows you to remain connected even when your phone is out of reach. Whether you're going for a run without your phone or you need to stay connected while on a trip, the **LTE model** ensures that you can make calls, send texts, and even stream music without needing to carry your smartphone.

Additionally, the ability to sync your **email**, **messages**, and **social media notifications** ensures that you are always in the loop. You can reply to text messages, answer calls, and check your calendar—all from the convenience of your wrist, which means you can be more productive without constantly checking your phone.

Samsung Pay and Smart Home Integration

With **Samsung Pay**, you can make secure, contactless payments directly from your wrist. This feature adds a layer of convenience when you're out shopping, dining, or handling transactions without the need for physical cards or cash.

The **Galaxy Watch5 Pro** also integrates seamlessly into the **Samsung SmartThings ecosystem**, allowing you to control smart home devices like lights, thermostats, and locks directly from the watch. Whether you're adjusting the thermostat from your wrist or turning off the lights while lying in bed, the watch makes managing your home more convenient and intuitive.

Exploring New Horizons with Outdoor Adventures

For those who love the outdoors, the **Galaxy Watch5 Pro** is a true adventurer's companion. Equipped with advanced GPS functionality, elevation tracking, and route navigation, it helps you explore new places with confidence, knowing that your watch is keeping track of your location and helping you find your way back if needed.

Navigation and Tracking

The **Galaxy Watch5 Pro** offers robust **GPS tracking**, allowing you to easily navigate unfamiliar terrain. Whether you're hiking, running, or cycling, the watch tracks your route and provides turn-by-turn directions, ensuring you stay on the right path. The **Track Back** feature also allows you to retrace your steps if you find yourself off course, offering peace of mind during your outdoor adventures.

In addition, the watch tracks **altitude and elevation**, which is perfect for those who enjoy mountain climbing, trail running, or any activity that requires tracking changes in altitude. With these features, the **Galaxy Watch5 Pro** enables you to push your limits while ensuring you're always aware of your surroundings.

Golf Mode and Other Sport Features

For sports enthusiasts, the **Galaxy Watch5 Pro** includes a **Golf Mode**, which offers features like course maps, distance tracking, and shot analysis. This makes it a great companion for avid golfers looking to improve their game. The watch also supports a variety of other sport-specific modes, including swimming, cycling, and running, giving you the tools to stay motivated and focused on your fitness goals.

Unmatched Customization and Personalization

One of the most appealing aspects of the **Galaxy Watch5 Pro** is its high level of **customization**. From the watch face to the straps, you can personalize every aspect of the watch to match your unique style and preferences.

Watch Faces and Strap Options

With the ability to choose from a variety of **watch faces**, you can change the look of your watch to suit any occasion or mood. Whether you prefer a classic analog look, a fitness-oriented face, or a minimalist design, the watch faces available on the **Galaxy Watch5 Pro** allow you to reflect your personal taste and needs.

You can also swap out the watch straps to match your style or for comfort. The **Galaxy Watch5 Pro** offers a variety of strap options, from sporty silicone bands for workouts to elegant leather straps for formal occasions. This flexibility allows you to make your watch as unique as you are.

Voice Commands and Smart Notifications

In addition to customizing the look of your watch, you can also **personalize** its functionality. With **Bixby**, Samsung's voice assistant, you can control the watch hands-free, whether you're checking the weather, setting a reminder, or starting a workout. The ability to use **voice commands** adds another layer of convenience, allowing you to interact with your watch while keeping your hands free.

Smart notifications keep you up to date on your important alerts, such as messages, calls, calendar events, and reminders. You can easily customize which notifications you want to receive and how they are delivered, ensuring you only see the things that matter most.

Troubleshooting and Maintenance Tips

While the **Samsung Galaxy Watch5 Pro** is designed to function seamlessly, you may occasionally encounter issues like syncing problems, connectivity glitches, or app crashes. Fortunately, the troubleshooting tips provided in this guide will help you resolve common issues quickly. Whether it's a software update, syncing issue, or Bluetooth problem, you'll be equipped with the knowledge to keep your watch running smoothly.

In addition, maintaining your watch is essential to ensuring it performs well over time. Regularly cleaning the watch, managing battery life, and performing updates will help keep the **Galaxy Watch5 Pro** functioning at its best. If you ever encounter an issue that can't be solved with troubleshooting,

Samsung's customer support is always available to assist you.

Looking Ahead: The Future with Your Galaxy Watch5 Pro

As you continue to use your **Galaxy Watch5 Pro**, you'll likely discover new features and ways to integrate the device into your lifestyle. Samsung regularly releases software updates that improve functionality, introduce new features, and enhance performance. By staying up to date with the latest updates, you'll ensure that your watch continues to evolve and adapt to your needs.

Additionally, as the world of wearable technology continues to grow, the **Galaxy Watch5 Pro** will remain a key player in helping you stay connected, healthy, and productive. With its seamless integration with Samsung's ecosystem, future features, and the ability to adapt to new advancements, your **Galaxy Watch5 Pro** will remain a reliable and versatile companion for years to come.

The **Samsung Galaxy Watch5 Pro** is more than just a smartwatch—it's a powerful tool designed to enhance every aspect of your life. Whether you're a fitness enthusiast, an adventurer, a busy professional, or someone simply looking to stay connected, the **Galaxy Watch5 Pro** has everything you need to help you achieve your goals.

With its **advanced health and fitness features, seamless integration with smart home technology, personalization options**, and **robust outdoor capabilities**, the **Galaxy Watch5 Pro** stands out as one of the most versatile and user-friendly wearables on the market today.

By following the steps outlined in this guide and continuing to explore the many features of your **Galaxy Watch5 Pro**, you'll be able to unlock its full potential and live your best, healthiest, and most connected life. Whether it's tracking your fitness, staying productive, or exploring new adventures, the **Galaxy Watch5 Pro** will always be there, helping you navigate and thrive in the modern world.

www.ingramcontent.com/pod-product-compliance
Lightning Source LLC
LaVergne TN
LVHW051342050326
832903LV00031B/3683

* 9 7 9 8 3 1 7 0 1 2 3 9 7 *